# BASIC MUSIC THEORY

## 50 Ready-to-Use Activities for Grades 3–9

UNIT 1

# BASIC MUSIC THEORY

## 50 Ready-to-Use Activities for Grades 3–9

*Audrey J. Adair*

*Illustrated by Leah Solsrud*

MUSIC CURRICULUM ACTIVITIES LIBRARY

**PARKER PUBLISHING COMPANY**
**West Nyack, New York 10994**

**Library of Congress Cataloging-in-Publication Data**

Adair, Audrey J.
Basic music theory.
ISBN 0-13-065707-7
(Music curriculum activities library ; unit 1)
1. School music—Instruction and study. 2. Music—Theory, Elementary. I. Title. II. Series: Adair, Audrey J., Music curriculum activities library ; unit 1.
MT10.A14 1987 unit 1
372.8'7 s 87-8828
[372.8'7]



*Printed in the United States of America*

11 12 13 14 15 16 17 18 19 20

ISBN 0-13-065707-7



**PARKER PUBLISHING COMPANY**
**West Nyack, New York 10994**

**On the World Wide Web at http://www.phdirect.com**

# About the Author

Audrey J. Adair has taught music at all levels in the Houston, Texas, and Dade County, Florida, public schools. She has served as a music consultant, music specialist, general music instructor, choir director, and classroom teacher. In addition, she has written a series of musical programs for assemblies and holiday events, conducted music workshops, organized music programs for the community, established glee club organizations, and done specialization work with gifted and special needs students. Currently, she directs and coordinates children's choirs, performs as soloist with flute as well as voice, and composes sacred music.

Mrs. Adair received her B.A. in Music Education from St. Olaf College in Northfield, Minnesota, and has done graduate work at the University of Houston and Florida Atlantic University in Fort Lauderdale. She is also the author of *Ready-to-Use Music Activities Kit* (Parker Publishing Company), a resource containing over 200 reproducible worksheets to teach basic music skills and concepts.

# About the *Library*

The *Music Curriculum Activities Library* was developed for you, the busy classroom teacher or music specialist, to provide a variety of interesting, well-rounded, step-by-step activities ready for use in your music classroom. The *Library*'s seven carefully planned Units combine imagination, motivation, and student involvement to make learning as exciting as going on a field trip and as easy as listening to music.

The units of the *Music Curriculum Activities Library* are designed to be used separately or in conjunction with each other. Each Unit contains 50 *all new* ready-to-use music activity sheets that can be reproduced as many times as needed for use by individual students. These 350 illustrated, easy-to-read activities will turn even your most reluctant students into eager learners. Each Unit offers a wealth of information on the following topics:

Unit 1: *Basic Music Theory* develops an understanding of the basic elements of melody, rhythm, harmony, and dynamics.

Unit 2: *Reading and Writing Music* provides a source of reinforcement and instills confidence in the beginner performer through a wide range of note-reading and writing activities in the treble clef, bass clef, and in the clef of one's own instrument.

Unit 3: *Types of Musical Form and Composition* gives the student the foundation needed to enjoy worthwhile music by becoming acquainted with a wide variety of styles and representative works.

Unit 4: *Musical Instruments and the Voice* provides knowledge of and insight into the characteristic sounds of band, orchestra, folk instruments, and the voice.

Unit 5: *Great Composers and Their Music* familiarizes the student with some of the foremost composers of the past and present and their music; and cultivates an early taste for good music.

Unit 6: *Special Days Throughout the Year* offers the student well-illustrated, music-related activities that stimulate interest and discussion about music through holidays and special occasions for the entire school year.

Unit 7: *Musicians in Action* helps the student examine music as a pastime or for a career by exploring daily encounters with music and the skills, duties, environment, and requirements of a variety of careers in music.

# How to Use the *Library*

The activities in each Unit of the *Library* may be sequenced and developed in different ways. The general teacher may want to use one activity after the other, while the music specialist may prefer to use the activities in conjunction with the sequencing of the music curriculum. Teachers with special or individualized needs may select activities from various Units and use them over and over before actually introducing new material.

Let's take a closer look at how you can use the *Music Curriculum Activities Library* in your particular classroom situation:

... For THE MUSIC TEACHER who is accountable for teaching classes at many grade levels, there is a wide range of activities with varying degrees of difficulty. The activity sheets are ideal to strengthen and review skills and concepts suitable for the general music class.

... For THE NEW TEACHER STARTING A GENERAL MUSIC CLASS, these fun-filled activities will provide a well-balanced, concrete core program.

... For THE SPECIALIZED TEACHER who needs to set definite teaching goals, these activities offer a wealth of information about certain areas of music, such as career awareness, composers, and musical forms.

... For THE BAND AND CHOIR DIRECTOR, these activity sheets are a valuable resource to explore band, orchestra, and folk instruments, along with the singing voice.

... For THE PRIVATE MUSIC TEACHER who wants to sharpen and improve students' note reading skills, the *Library* offers ample homework assignments to give students the additional practice they need. There are many activity sheets using the clef of one's instrument and theory pages with illustrations of the keyboard.

... For THE MUSIC CONSULTANT using any one of the units, there are plenty of activities specifically correlated to the various areas of music providing reinforcement of learning. The activity sheets are suitable for class adoption in correlation with any music book series.

... For THE THEORY TEACHER, there are activities to show the students that music analysis is fun and easy.

... For THE TEACHER WHO NEEDS AN ADEQUATE MEANS OF EVALUATING STUDENT PROGRESS, there are fact-filled activities ideal for diagnostic purposes. A space is provided on each sheet for a score to be given.

. . . For THE CLASSROOM TEACHER with little or no musical background, the *Library* offers effective teaching with the flexibility of the seven units. All that has to be done is to decide on the music skill or concept to be taught and then duplicate the necessary number of copies. Even the answers can be duplicated for self-checking.

. . . For THE SUBSTITUTE TEACHER, these sheets are ideal for seatwork assignments because the directions are generally self-explanatory with minimal supervision required.

. . . For THE INSTRUCTOR OF GIFTED STUDENTS, the activities may be used for any type of independent, individualized instruction and learning centers. When used in an individualized fashion, the gifted student has an opportunity to pursue music learning at his or her own pace.

. . . For THE TEACHER OF SPECIAL EDUCATION, even the disadvantaged and remedial student can get in on the fun. Each concept or skill will be mastered as any lesson may be repeated or reinforced with another activity. Some of these activity sheets are designed to provide success for students who have difficulty in other subject areas.

. . . For the INDIVIDUAL who desires to broaden and expand his or her own knowledge and interest in music, each Unit provides 50 activities to help enjoy music.

The *Music Curriculum Activities Library* is ideally a teacher's program because a minimum of planning is required. A quick glance at the Contents in each Unit reveals the titles of all the activity sheets, the ability level necessary to use them, and the skills involved for each student. Little knowledge of music is generally needed to introduce the lessons, and extensive preparation is seldom necessary. You will, of course, want to read through the activity before presenting it to the class. In cases where you need to give information about the activity, two different approaches might be considered. (1) Use the activity as a basis for a guided discussion before completing the activity to achieve the desired results, or (2) Use the activity as a foundation for a lesson plan and then follow up by completing the activity. Either one of these approaches will enhance your own and your students' confidence and, by incorporating a listening or performing experience with this directed study, the students will have a well-rounded daily lesson.

All activity sheets throughout the *Library* have the same format. They are presented in an uncluttered, easy-to-read fashion, with self-explanatory directions. You need no extra materials or equipment, except for an occasional pair of scissors. The classroom or resource area should, however, contain a few reference books, such as song books or music series' books, encyclopedias, reference books about composers, a dictionary, music dictionary or glossary, and so on, so that while working on certain activities the student has easy access to resource books. Then, you simply need to duplicate the activity sheet as many times as needed and give a copy to each student. Even paper grading can be kept to a minimum by reproducing the answer key for self-checking.

The collection of activities includes practice in classifying, matching, listing, researching, naming, drawing, decoding, identifying, doing picture or crossword puzzles, anagrams, word searches, musical word squares, and much much more.

These materials may be used successfully with students in grades 3 and up. The activities and artwork are intentionally structured to appeal to a wide range of ages. For this reason, no grade-level references appear on the activity sheets so that you can use them in a variety of classroom settings, although suggested ability levels (beginner, intermediate, advanced) appear in the Contents.

The potential uses for the *Library* for any musical purpose (or even interdisciplinary study) are countless. Why? Because these activities allow you to instruct an entire class, a smaller group within the classroom, or individual students. While you are actively engaged in teaching one group of students, the activity sheets may be completed by another group. In any kind of classroom setting, even with the gifted music student or the remedial child, no student needs to sit idle. Now you will have more time for individual instruction.

The Units may be used in a comprehensive music skills program, in an enrichment program, or even in a remedial program. The *Library* is perfect for building a comprehensive musicianship program, improving basic music skills, teaching career awareness, building music vocabulary, exploring instruments, developing good taste in listening to music, appreciating different types of music, creating a positive learning environment, and providing growing confidence in the performer.

# What Each Unit Offers You

A quick examination of the **Contents** will reveal a well balanced curriculum. Included are the titles of all activities, the level of difficulty, and the skill involved. The exception to this is Unit 6, where the date and special day, rather than the skill, are listed with the title of each activity.

Each of the **50 reproducible activity sheets** generally presents a single idea, with a consistent format and easy-to-follow directions on how to do the activity, along with a sufficient amount of material to enable the student to become proficient through independent and self-directed work. Because each activity has but one single behavioral objective, mastery of each skill builds confidence that allows the learner to continue progressively toward a more complete understanding of the structure of music, appreciation of music, and its uses. The activity sheets are just the right length, too, designed to be completed within a class period.

The **Progress Chart** provides a uniform, objective method of determining what skills have been mastered. With the aid of this chart, you will be able to keep track of goals, set priorities, organize daily and weekly lesson plans, and track assignments. The Progress Chart lists each activity and skill involved, and has a space for individual names or classes to be recorded and checked when each activity and skill is complete. The Progress Chart is ideal for accurate record keeping. It provides a quick, sure method for you to determine each individual student's achievements or weaknesses.

Use the **Teacher's Guide** for practical guidance on how the particular Unit will work for you. An easy effective learning system, this guide provides background information and reveals new techniques for teaching the Unit.

Throughout the *Library*, each **Answer Key** is designed with a well-thought-out system for checking students' answers. While some activities are self-checking without the use of the Answer Key, other activities can easily be student corrected, too, by simply duplicating the answer page and cutting apart the answers by activity number.

**The Self-Improvement Chart** provides the student with a self-assessment system that links curriculum goals with individual goals. By means of an appraisal checklist, the chart gives the student and teacher alike the key to finding individual talent. It also measures accountability. Included in the chart are (1) a method for recording goals and acquired music skills; (2) a log for attendance at special music events; (3) a music and instrument check-out record; (4) a log for extra credit activities and music projects; (5) a record of special music recognition awards, incentive badges, Music Share-a-Grams, Return-a-Grams; and (6) a record of music progress.

These specific features of the chart will help you:

- Provide a uniform, objective method of determining rewards for students.
- Assess future curriculum needs by organizing long-term information on student performance.
- Foster understanding of why students did or did not qualify for additional merit.
- Motivate students by giving them feedback on ways for self-improvement.
- Assist students in making statements of their own desires and intentions for learning, and in checking progress toward their goals.

The **Music Share-a-Gram** is a personalized progress report addressed to the parent and created to show the unique qualities of the individual child. It allows you to pinpoint areas of success and tell parents what they need to know about their child. The Music Share-a-Gram evaluates twelve important abilities and personal traits with ratings from exceptional to unsatisfactory, which you might want to discuss with students to solicit their reaction. For example, you might use these ratings as a basis for selecting a student to attend the gifted program in music. This form is designed to be sent with or without the Return-a-Gram, and may be hand-delivered by the student or sent through the mail. For easy record keeping, make a copy of the Gram and attach it to the back of the Student Record Profile Chart.

The **Return-a-Gram** is designed to accompany the Music Share-a-Gram and is sent to the parent on special occasions. When a reply is not expected or necessary, simply detach the Return-a-Gram before sending the Share-a-Gram. This form encourages feedback from the parent and even allows the parent to arrange for a parent-teacher conference. Both Grams are printed on the same page and are self-explanatory—complete with a dotted line for the parent to detach, fill in, and return.

The **Student Record Profile Chart** is a guide for understanding and helping students, and offers a means of periodic evaluation. The chart is easy to use and provides all you need for accurate record keeping and measuring accountability for individual student progress throughout all seven units. It provides an accumulative skills profile for the student and represents an actual score of his or her written performance for each activity. Here is a workable form that you can immediately tailor to your own requirements for interpretation and use of scores. Included are clear instructions, with an example, to help you record your students' assessment on a day-to-day basis, to keep track of pupil progress, and to check learning patterns over a period of time. This chart allows you to spot the potential superior achiever along with the remedial individual. The chart coordinates all aspects of data ranging from the students' name, class, school, classroom teacher's name, semester, date, page number, actual grade, and attendance.

The **Word List** is presented as a reinforcement for building a music vocabulary. It emphasizes the use of dictionary skills; the students make a glossary of important words related to the particular unit. Its purpose is to encourage the use of vocabulary skills by helping develop an understanding of the music terms, concepts, and names found on the activity sheets. This vocabulary reference page is meant to be reproduced and used by the individual student throughout the units as a guide for spelling, word recognition, pronunciation, recording definitions, plus any other valuable information. Throughout six units of the *Library*, a cumulation of the words are presented on the Word List pages. (A Word List is not included in Unit 6.) With the help of this extensive vocabulary, when the student uses the words on both the activity page and the Word List, they will become embedded as part of his or her language.

Each Unit contains a wide-ranging collection of **Incentive Badges**. Use them to reward excellence, commend effort, for bonuses, prizes, behavior modification, or as reminders. These badges are designed to capture the interest and attention of the entire school. Several badges are designed with an open-ended format to provide maximum flexibility in meeting any special music teaching requirement.

Included in each Unit is a simple **Craft Project** that may be created by the entire class or by individual students. Each craft project is an integral part of the subject matter of that particular unit and will add a rich dimension to the activities. The materials necessary for the construction of the craft projects have been limited to those readily available in most classrooms and call for no special technical or artistic skills.

**PLUS** each Unit contains:

- Worked-out sample problems for students to use as a standard and model for their own work.
- Additional teaching suggestions in the Answer Key for getting the most out of certain activities.
- Extra staff paper for unlimited use, such as composing, ear training, improvising, or writing chords.
- Activities arranged in a sequential pattern.

# Resources for Teaching Music More Effectively

- Have a classroom dictionary available for reference.
- Have a glossary or music dictionary available for reference.
- Use only one activity sheet per class session.
- Distribute the Word List prior to the first activity sheet of the particular unit. Encourage students to underline familiar words on the list and write definitions or identifications on the back before instruction on the unit begins. Later, the students can compare their answers with those studied.
- Provide short-term goals for each class session and inform students in advance that awards will be given for the day. You'll see how their conduct improves, too.
- Encourage students to make or buy an inexpensive folder to store music activity sheets, craft projects, word lists, self-evaluation charts, and so on. Folders might be kept in the classroom when not in use and distributed at the beginning of each class period.
- Many of the activities are ideal for bulletin board display. If space is not available to display all students' work, rotate the exhibits.
- Encourage students to re-read creative writing pages for clarity and accuracy before copying the final form on the activity sheet. Proofreading for grammatical and spelling errors should be encouraged.
- For creative drawing activities, encourage students to sketch their initial ideas on another sheet of paper first, then draw the finished product on the activity sheet. It is not necessary to have any technical ability in drawing to experience the pleasure of these creative activities.
- Although you will probably want to work through parts of some activities with your students, and choose some activities for group projects, you will find that most lessons are designed to lead students to the correct answers with little or no teacher direction. Students can be directed occasionally to work through an activity with a partner to search out and correct specific errors.
- Self-corrections and self-checking make a much better impression on young learners than do red-penciled corrections by the classroom music teacher.
- On activities where answers will vary, encourage students to rate their own work on correctness, originality, completeness, carefulness, realism, and organization.

• Most activity pages will serve as a "teacher assistant" in developing specific skills or subject areas to study. The activities throughout the series are complete with learning objectives and are generally factual enough for the teacher to use as a basis for a daily lesson plan.

• The library research activities promote creativity instead of copying while students search out relevant data from a variety of sources, such as encyclopedias, dictionaries, reference books, autobiographies, and others. These activities are ideal for the individual student or groups of students working beyond the classroom environment.

• The following are practical guidelines in planning, organizing, and constructing the Craft Projects:

. . . Acquaint yourself with any of the techniques that are new to you before you ask your students to undertake the project.

. . . Decide on your project and assemble the materials before you begin.

. . . Make a sample model for experience.

. . . Use a flat surface for working.

. . . Be sure the paper is cut exactly to measurements and that folds are straight.

. . . Be available for consultation.

. . . Provide guidance on what the next logical step is to encourage all students to finish their projects.

. . . Use the finished craft projects as displays and points of interest for your school's open house.

• Many of the Incentive Badges found in each Unit are open-ended and can be made effective communication tools to meet your needs. Extra space is provided on these badges for additional written messages that might be used for any number of reasons. Be creative for your own special needs; load the copier with colored paper and print as many as you need for the semester or entire school year. Then simply use a paper cutter to separate the badges and sort them out alphabetically. Make an alphabetical index on file card dividers using these titles. Next, arrange them in an accessible file box or shoe box, depending on the size needed. Include a roll of tape to attach the badge to the recipient.

# Teacher's Guide to Unit 1

*Basic Music Theory* is divided into six parts covering the basic elements in music theory: pitch, intervals, dynamics, duration, keys and scales, and music terminology. The 50 activity sheets in Unit 1 will help your students learn the basics in music and will provide them with lessons that offer a variety of motivating musical experiences that are fun. These activity sheets were not created to introduce new material, but to reinforce and review the basic fundamentals of music in a novel way. For this information about music facts, terminology, symbols, and concepts to be valid, the activities are best used in conjunction with listening and performing experiences—the only way this knowledge will relate to music.

All of the information in Unit 1 is basic to the general curriculum. Be sure you provide continuity from one class session to the next while presenting music theory. As students feel they are accomplishing something and moving forward, they will gain confidence. Theory must not be presented as a collection of worksheets, but as an exciting discovery of how music is structured. Use these activity sheets in conjunction with listening experiences and realize that learning music theory is a very slow process. Be patient and go with the pace of the class. Interest in music theory may grow very slowly, and the results are difficult to measure. Encourage beginning note readers to use the Study Guide Strips, a special feature of Unit 1 found after the Answer Key. These three strips illustrate and name note placement on the Treble (G) staff, the Bass (F) staff, and the Grand staff with keyboard, and may be used by students while completing an activity, as a device for self-checking, or simply as a pocket study guide.

Help the students work toward a definite goal. Keep completed theory activity sheets in individual notebooks. These notebooks will help the students review the material already learned.

# Contents

# Activities for Learning PITCH

Name ______________________________ Score ________

Date ______________________________ Class ________

## TREBLE KROSS 1-1

Circle all words in the square going across and down using only letters of the music alphabet. Then write nine of the words below in any order and draw the matching notes directly above each word on the staff. An example is given.

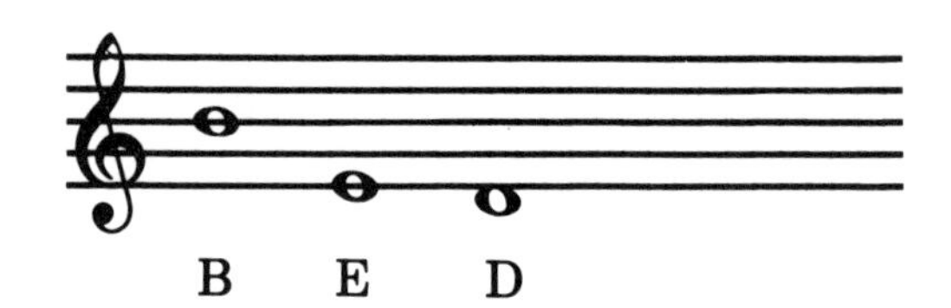


| | | | | | | | | |
|---|---|---|---|---|---|---|---|---|
| B | E | D | E | X | F | A | C | E |
| B | L | M | Y | E | Y | Z | M | D |
| D | E | E | D | Q | M | U | P | G |
| O | P | M | W | M | C | U | Z | E |
| C | A | U | B | E | A | D | R | Y |
| A | B | L | I | L | B | S | E | L |
| F | R | U | N | C | B | Q | M | P |
| E | W | X | O | T | A | G | E | D |
| I | O | P | C | A | G | E | D | M |
| L | B | A | D | G | E | J | K | S |

1. 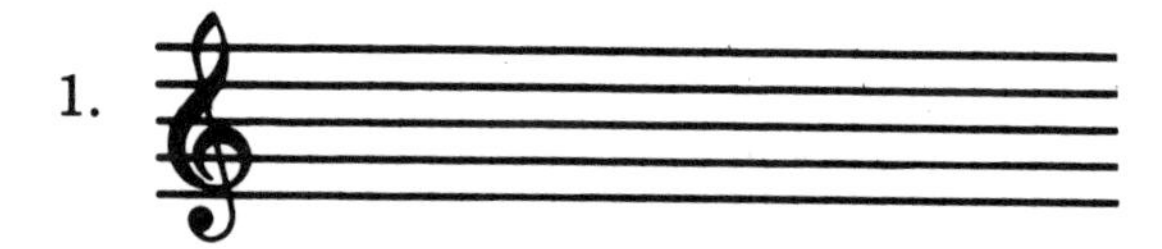

2. 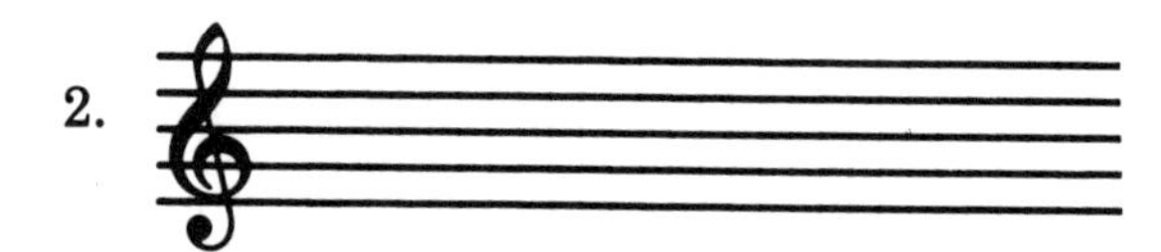

3. 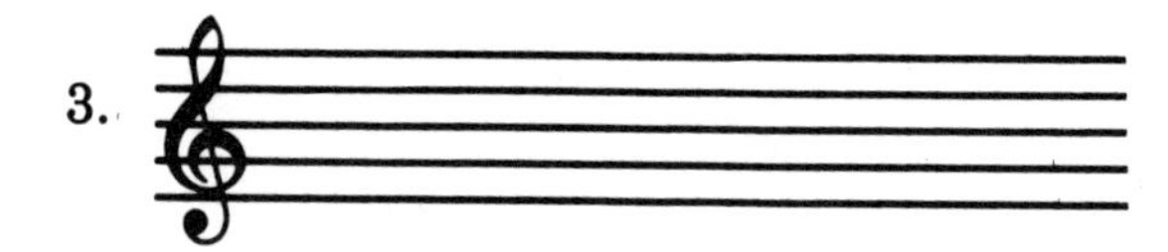

4. 

5. 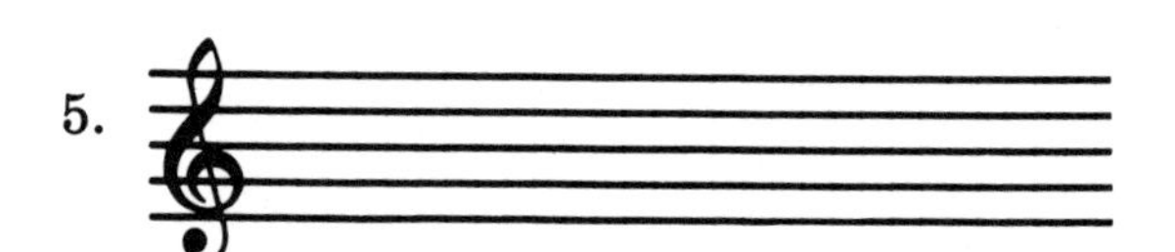

6.

7.

8.

9. 

Name ____________________ Score ________

Date ____________________ Class ________

## TREBLE PICTURE PUZZLES

1–2

The names of these pictures use only letters from the music alphabet. Solve the puzzles by printing the names of the pictures under the staffs. Then carefully draw notes on the staffs to match the letters. An example is given.

| Example | 1 | 2 |
|---|---|---|
|  b e a d | | |
| **3** | **4** | **5** TAXI |
| **6** LEMON ___ 10¢ | **7** | **8** |

Name ______________________________ Score ________

Date ______________________________ Class ________

## BASS KROSS 1–3

Circle all words in the square going across and down using only letters of the music alphabet. Then write eight of the words below in any order and draw the matching notes directly above each word on the staff. An example is given.

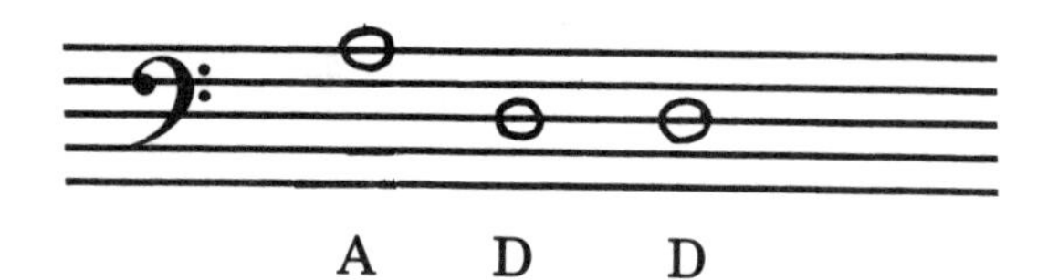


| | | | | | | | | |
|---|---|---|---|---|---|---|---|---|
| A | D | D | O | L | N | R | T | Z |
| L | P | Y | B | E | G | G | E | D |
| M | C | R | Y | D | V | O | F | N |
| W | A | S | G | C | O | I | A | R |
| M | B | I | C | A | F | E | D | Y |
| S | B | I | M | G | K | Z | E | S |
| J | A | N | D | E | E | D | M | X |
| D | G | T | S | Y | U | R | Y | P |
| A | E | M | P | L | B | E | E | F |
| B | Z | W | D | B | A | D | G | E |

1.

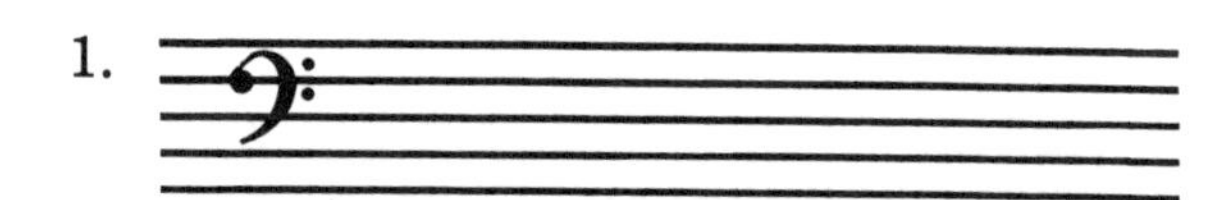

2.

3.

4.

5.

6.

7.

8.

Name ______________________ Score ________

Date ______________________ Class ________

# BASS PICTURE PUZZLES

1-4

The names of these pictures use only letters from the music alphabet. Solve the puzzles by printing the names of the pictures under the staffs. Then carefully draw notes on the staffs to match the letters. An example is given.

| Example | 1 | 2 |
| --- | --- | --- |
| c a g e | 2 +3 5 | |
| **3** | **4** | **5** |
| POLICE | | |
| **6** | **7** | **8** |
| TAXI | | A A |

Name ______________________ Score __________

Date ______________________ Class __________

## KEYS 'N' NOTES

1–5

Shown here is part of a piano keyboard with the bass and treble staff. Finish writing the letter names on the white keys of the keyboard. Then draw the matching notes on the staffs. Connect the notes with the keys as shown.

Name ____________________ Score ________

Date ____________________ Class ________

## BE ON THE LOOKOUT!

1–6

Two or more measures on each staff are repeated. Find the repeated measures and circle them as in the example.

Name ______________________________ Score ________

Date ______________________________ Class ________

## YOU FIGURE OUT THE DIRECTION 1-7

Look at the arrow above each keyboard to decide which direction the keys should be played ( ⇦ = right to left, ⇨ = left to right). Draw whole notes in the proper direction and in the correct order on the staffs.

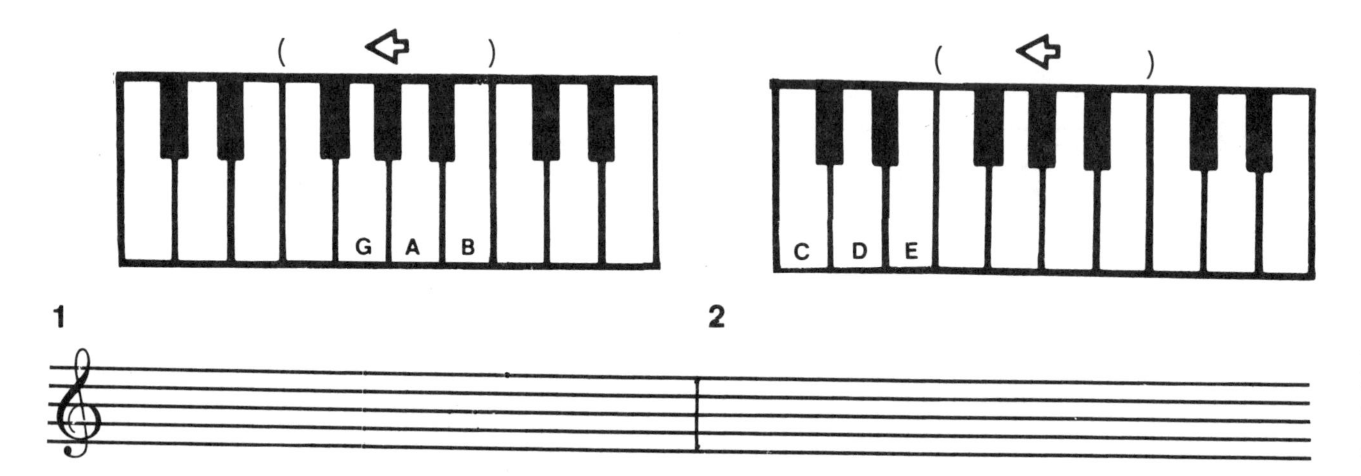


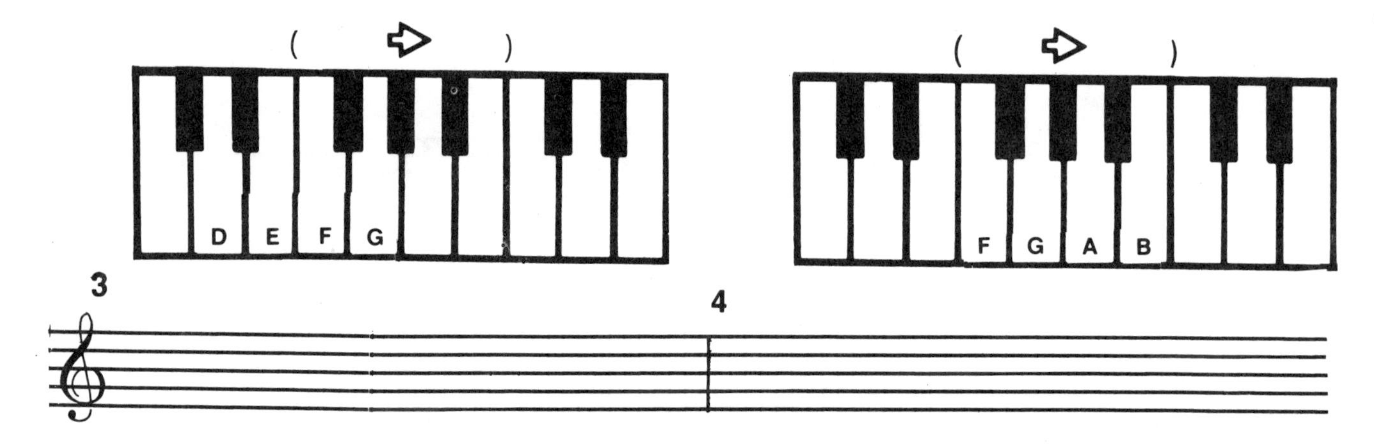

Name ____________________ Score ________

Date ____________________ Class ________

## FINISH THE SEQUENCE 1-8

Draw the clef of *your* instrument at the beginning of each staff. Then continue to repeat the melodic phrase at the next pitch level. An example is given.

Name ______________________ Score ________

Date ______________________ Class ________

## REARRANGE THE NOTES 1–9

Notes with only three letter names were used in the song "Taps." That tune is an example of how only a few notes can be used in a composition.

**Part One:**

Three notes can be arranged in six different ways. One way is shown here. Try to arrange the notes in five other ways. Write the letter names under the staff.

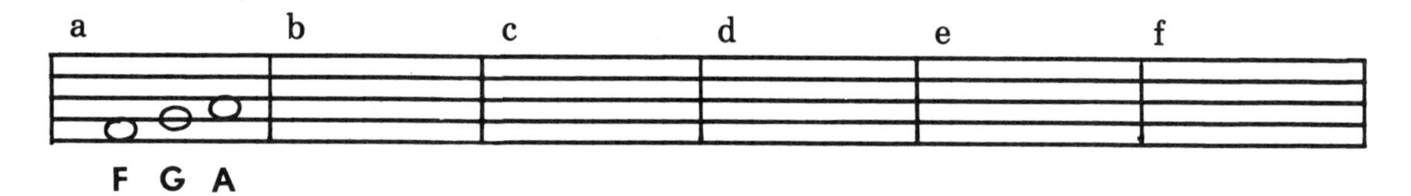


**Part Two:**

Four notes can be arranged twenty-four different ways. Use the notes C, D, E and G to compose twenty-three more patterns. Write the letter names under the notes.

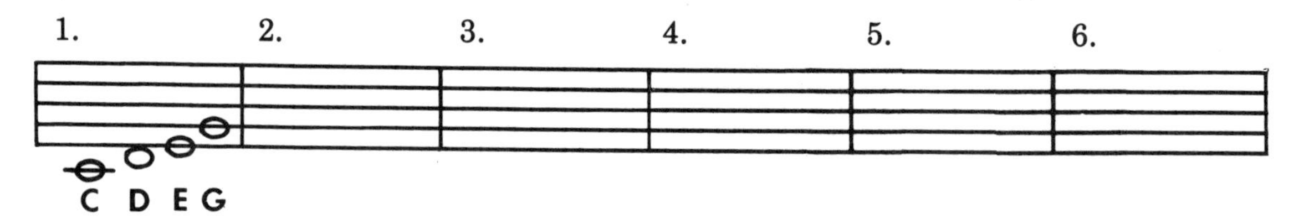


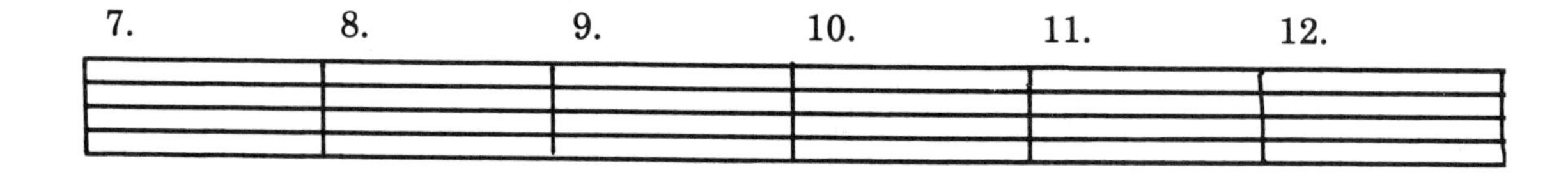


13. 14. 15. 16. 17. 18.

19. 20. 21. 22. 23. 24.

Name ______________________________ Score __________

Date ______________________________ Class __________

## TRANSCRIBE A TUNE 1–10

A performer needs this tune pitched higher. Use the same rhythm as in the original song and use the letter names under the staff for the correct notes. The first measure is given. Finish writing the song.

### This Old Man

Key of A Major

Key of C Major

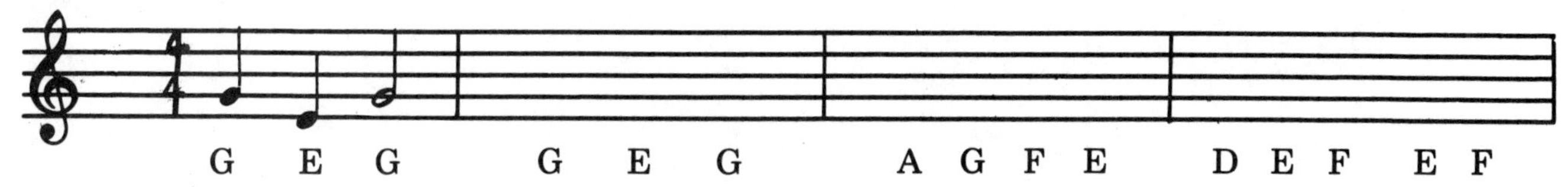


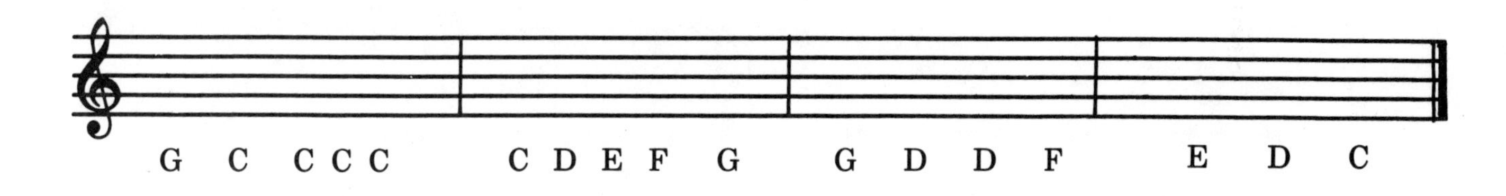

Name ______________________ Score ________

Date ______________________ Class ________

## CHORD CLUES

1–11

Draw a chord in each measure to match the circled notes on the keyboard. Analyze the chords and write the Key Signatures on the blanks.

1 Key of ______

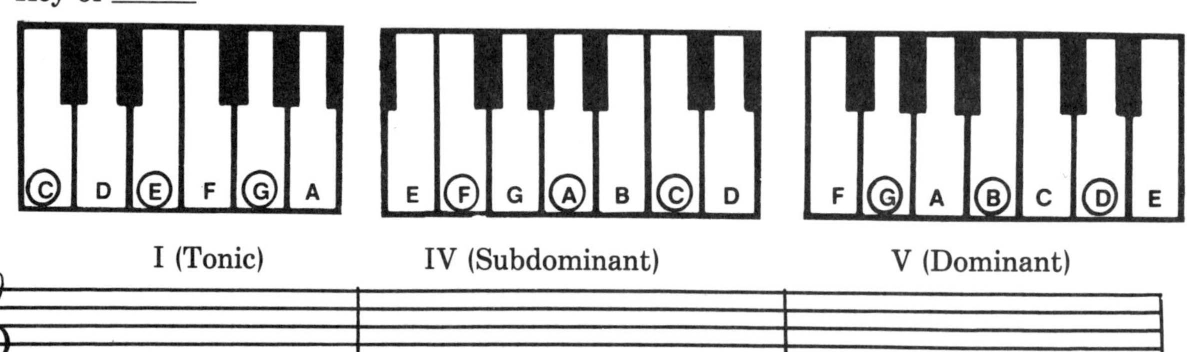


2 Key of ______

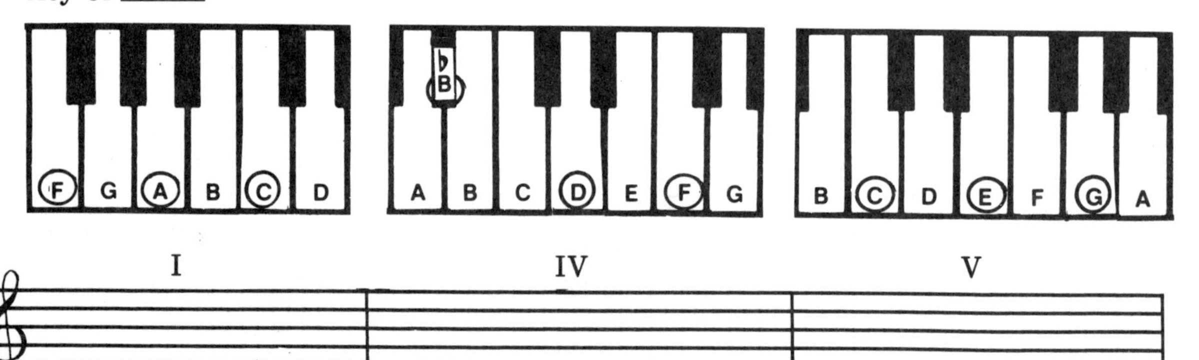


Write the letter names on the keys to match the chords below.

3 Key of ______

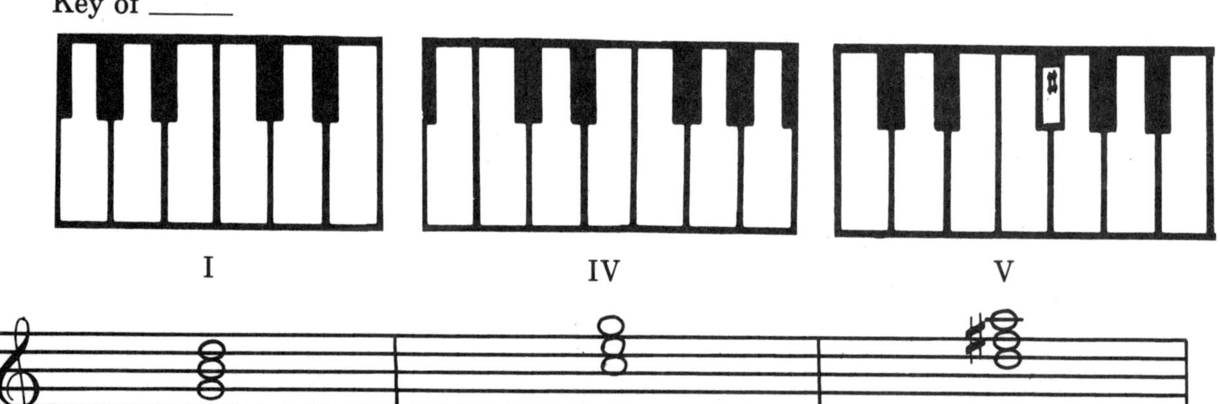

# Activities for Learning
# INTERVALS

Name ______________________ Score ________

Date ______________________ Class ________

## WRITE THE INTERVAL

1–12

Study the examples for different types of intervals used on this page. Then draw the correct note on the staff and write the matching letter name on the blank.

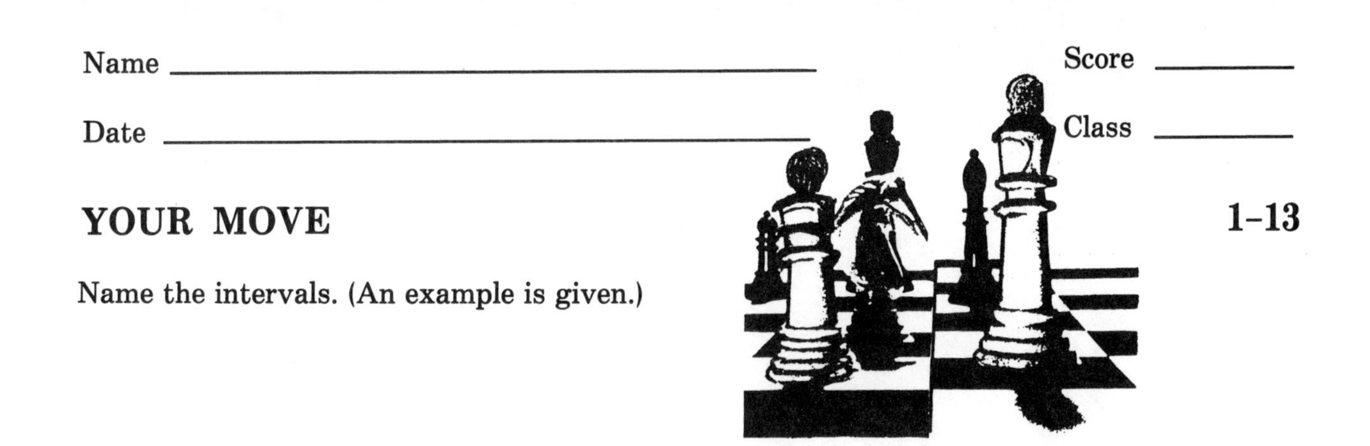

Name ________________________ Score ________

Date ________________________ Class ________

## YOUR MOVE

1-13

Name the intervals. (An example is given.)

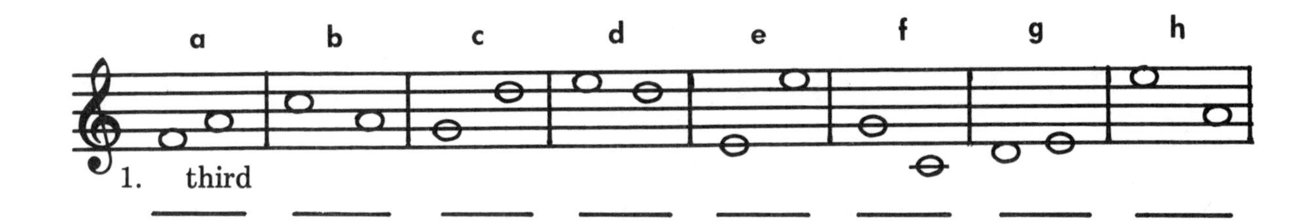

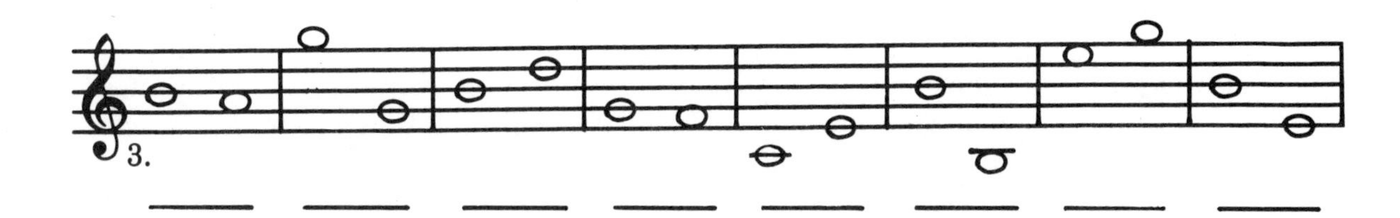


Draw the higher note of each interval as indicated.

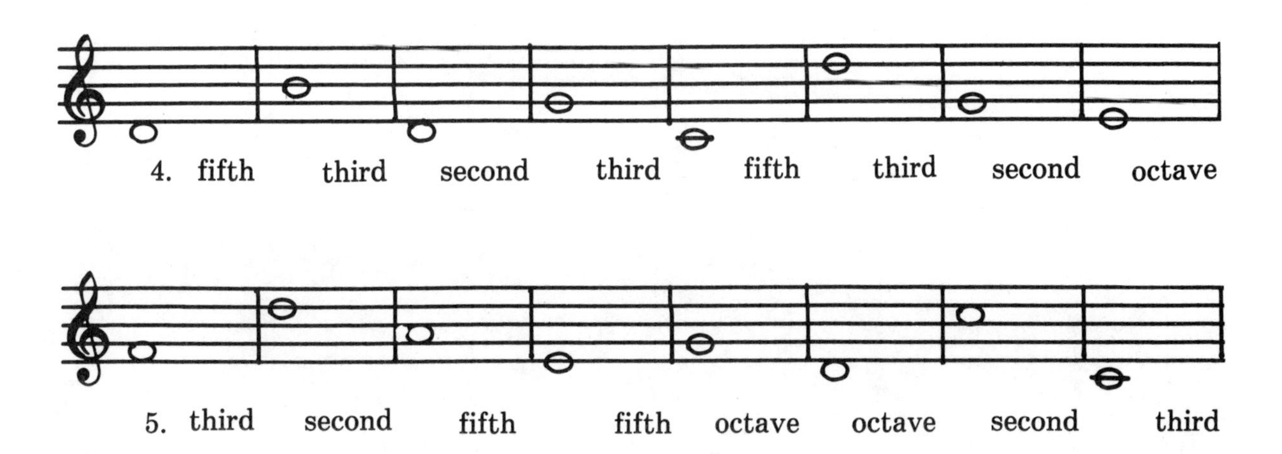

# Activities for Learning
# DYNAMICS

Name ______________________

Date ______________________

Score ________

Class ________

# MATCH THE SPEED

1–14

Below is a list of common tempo markings and their meanings. Choose four different tempos ranging *in order* from slow to fast and write the Italian names on the blanks as they appear below. Then draw a stick man in a walking position or running position to match the speed in the appropriate box.

1. PRESTISSIMO – as fast as possible
2. PRESTO – very rapidly
3. ALLEGRO – quick, lively
4. ANDANTE – a slow, even tempo
5. LENTO – a slow tempo, between ADAGIO and ANDANTE
6. ADAGIO – slower than andante
7. LARGO – slow broad tempo
8. GRAVE – the slowest musical tempo

Name ____________________ Score ________

Date ____________________ Class ________

## CLASSIFY THE DYNAMICS

**1-15**

Music has different levels of loudness depending on its feeling or mood. For example, "Cradle Song" would be sung softly, while "Yankee Doodle" would be sung much louder. The composer usually indicates how loud or soft a piece should be played or sung by using dynamics. The signs, along with their matching Italian names, are listed here in order from "As loud as possible" to "As soft as possible." Draw the signs and write the Italian names in the same order beside the definitions on the chart below.

1. ***fff*** Fortississimo
2. ***ff*** Fortissimo
3. ***f*** Forte
4. ***mf*** Mezzo-forte
5. ***sf*** Sforzando
6. ***m*** Mezzo
7. ***mp*** Mezzo-piano
8. ***p*** Piano
9. ***pp*** Pianissimo
10. ***ppp*** Pianississimo

| | | | DYNAMICS |
|---|---|---|---|
| | **Sign or Symbol** | **Name** | **Definition** |
| 1. | | | As loud as possible |
| 2. | | | Very loud |
| 3. | | | Loud |
| 4. | | | Moderately loud |
| 5. | | | Forced, accented |
| 6. | | | Medium; the middle; half |
| 7. | | | Moderately soft |
| 8. | | | Soft |
| 9. | | | Very soft |
| 10. | | | As soft as possible |

Name ______________________ Score ________

Date ______________________ Class ________

## EXPRESS THE TENSION 1–16

When music becomes louder it often causes more tension. Dynamics obviously are an important part of musical expression. The dynamic marks or expression marks in a song are only relative, because how the performer plays or sings a song depends on his or her artistic judgment. It's not uncommon to hear a piece played at different levels by different performers.

Listed below are changes of expression in dynamics in order from "Loud to soft" to "Gradually diminishing in power." Draw the signs and write the Italian names in the same order beside the definitions in the chart.

| | | |
|---|---|---|
| 1. | *fp* | Forte-piano |
| 2. | *sf* | Sforzato |
| 3. | < > | Messa di voce |
| 4. | < | Crescendo ( *cresc.* ) |
| 5. | > | Decrescendo ( *decresc.* ) |
| 6. | > | Diminuendo (dim.) |

### CHANGES OF EXPRESSION IN DYNAMICS

| | Sign or Symbol | Name | Definition |
|---|---|---|---|
| 1. | | | Loud to soft |
| 2. | | | Forced, accented |
| 3. | | | A gradual swelling and subsiding on a single tone in singing or playing |
| 4. | | | Gradually increasing in power |
| 5. | | | Gradually diminishing in power |
| 6. | | | Gradually diminishing in power |

# Activities for Learning
# DURATION

Name ______________________ Score __________

Date ______________________ Class __________

## FIND THE LOOK-ALIKES

1–17

Circle the matching notes and then name them.

| | a | b | c | d | e |
|---|---|---|---|---|---|
| Example: | | | | quarter | |
| 1. | | | | | |
| 2. | | | | | |
| 3. | | | | | |
| 4. | | | | | |
| 5. | | | | | |

Name ______________________________ Score ________

Date ______________________________ Class ________

## HELP THE MUSIC MONSTER

1–18

Help the music monster solve the problem. Place the correct notes in the empty squares in order to get the answers shown.

NOTE KEY:

- ♪ = ½ count
- ♩ = 1 count
- 𝅗𝅥 = 2 counts
- 𝅝 = 4 counts

Name ______________________________

Date ______________________________

Score __________

Class __________

## TAKE A REST

1–19

Circle the rests to match the notes and then, below the circled rests, name them. Select your answers from the following: whole, half, quarter, eighth, sixteenth.

| | a | b | c | d | e |
|---|---|---|---|---|---|
| 1. 𝅝 | 𝄽 | 𝄼 | 𝄾 | 𝄻 | 𝄼 |
| 2. 𝅗𝅥 | 𝄼 | 𝄽 | 𝄻 | 𝄾 | 𝄼 |
| 3. 𝅘𝅥 | 𝄾 | 𝄿 | 𝄽 | 𝄼 | 𝄽 |
| 4. 𝅘𝅥𝅮 | 𝄽 | 𝄾 | 𝄼 | 𝄾 | 𝄿 |
| 5. 𝅘𝅥𝅯 | 𝄽 | 𝄻 | 𝄼 | 𝄽 | 𝄿 |

Name ______________________________ Score ________

Date ______________________________ Class ________

## COMPUTING RESTS 1–20

Use the numbers from the computer printout to complete the answers.

1. For every note there is ____ rest to equal it.
2. A whole note rest is held for ____ count(s).
3. A half note rest is held for ____ beat(s).
4. A quarter note rest is held for ____ count(s).
5. An eighth note rest is held for ____ count(s).
6. If a whole note rest equals 4 counts, then a half note rest will equal ____ count(s).
7. If a quarter note is held for one beat, then a quarter note rest will equal ____ count(s).
8. One 𝄽 = ________ quarter note(s).
9. One 𝄼 = ________ half note(s).
10. One 𝄾 = ________ eighth note(s).
11. One 𝅝 = ________ whole rest(s).
12. One 𝅗𝅥 = ________ quarter rest(s).
13. One 𝄽 = ________ eighth note(s).
14. One 𝄻 = ________ quarter note(s).

Computer Printout

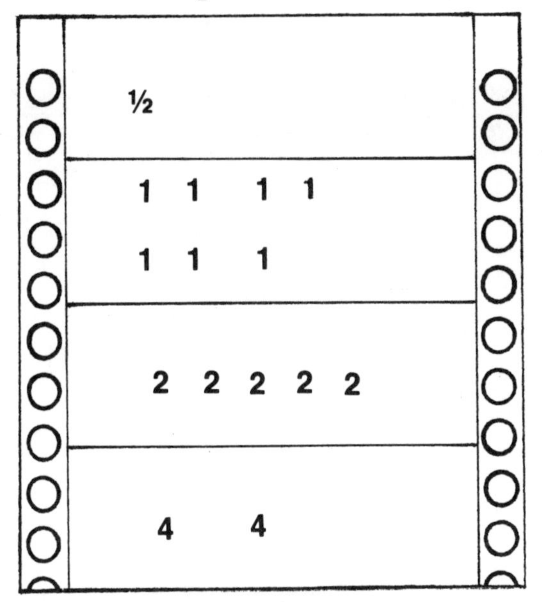

Name ______________________________ Score ________

Date ______________________________ Class ________

## MARK THE MEASURES

1–21

The music typist forgot to divide this song into measures. Finish this composition by adding the bar lines.

**Old MacDonald**

Name ______________________________  Score ________

Date ______________________________  Class ________

## FINISH THE MEASURES

1–22

Look at the Time Signatures and complete the measures by adding the number of notes indicated in the circle. Check the stem direction.

a b c d

1. (1)

4/4

2. (2)

4/4

3. (1)

3/4

4. (2)

3/4

5. (1)

2/4

Name ______________________ Score ________

Date ______________________ Class ________

## YOU CALL THE TIME

1–23

Write the Meter Signature at the beginning of each set of measures.

1. 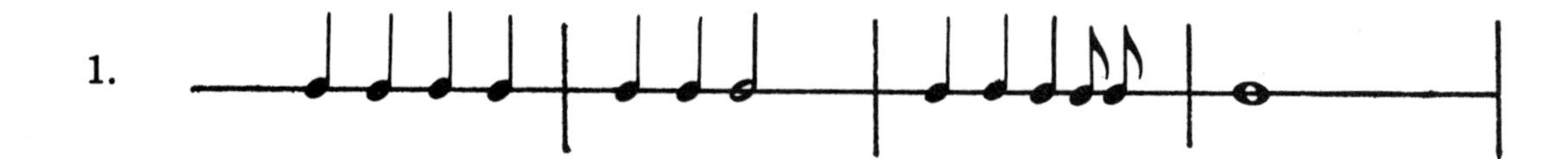

2.

3.

4.

5.

6.

7.

8.

Name ______________________________ Score ________

Date ______________________________ Class ________

## WRITE THE RHYTHM

1–24

As you read each sentence below, tap the rhythm. Record the rhythm on the staff line above the set of words. Then draw the bar lines and write the appropriate Meter Signature. An example is given.

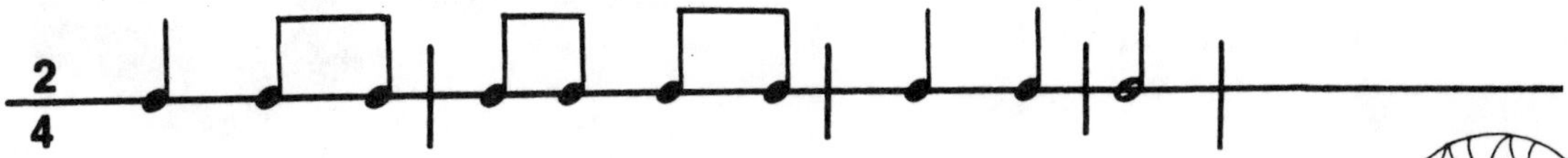

Example: How man - y jack-o- lan- terns did you see?

1. Go to sleep be-fore the sun comes up.

2. Tick, tock, tick, tock, hear the clock!

3. Lis-ten to the mo-tor-cy-cle roar; roar.

4. Fire in the en-gine, fire down be-low.

5. Boom, boom, beat the drum!

6. Lem-on-ade, lem-on-ade, fif-teen cents!

Name ______________________________ Score __________

Date ______________________________ Class __________

## WHAT'S THE TIME?

1–25

Below are the beginning measures of five well-known songs. Each is missing the Time Signature and the title. First, write the note values under the staff. (For example ♩ = 1 count.) Then write the Time Signature after the Treble Clef sign. After you have finished, guess the name of the song from the list below and write the title above the staff.

1.
Count:

2.
Count:

3.
Count:

4.
Count:

5.
Count:

**Song Titles**

"Mary Had a Little Lamb"
"Go Tell Aunt Rhodie"
"Blow the Man Down"
"Lowly Brays the Donkey"
"Oh Where Has My Little Dog Gone?"

Name ______________________ Score ________

Date ______________________ Class ________

## COMPOSE AN OSTINATO 1–26

Here is an example of a simple ostinato pattern that can be used to accompany the song "Are You Sleeping?"

Note Key: Name of Instrument: Triangle

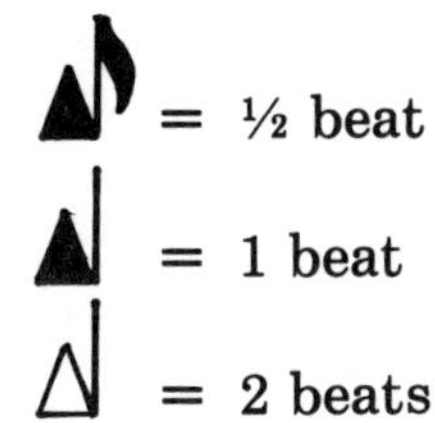


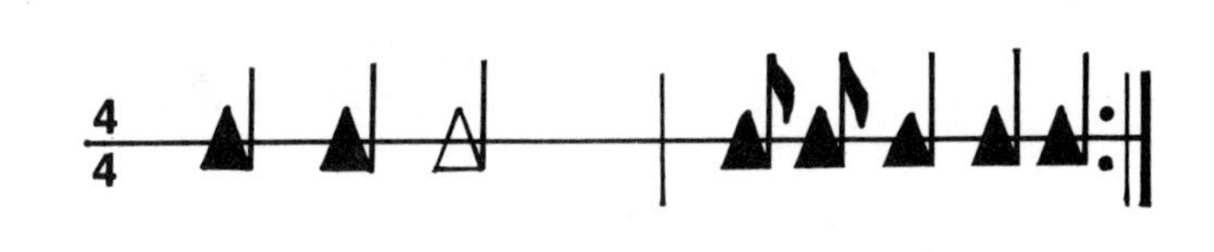


**Are You Sleeping?**

Select an appropriate percussion instrument and write a simple repeated rhythmic pattern for this song. Make up your own symbols for notation.

Note Key: Name of Instrument:

Name ______________________________ Score __________

Date ______________________________ Class __________

## FINISH THE UNFINISHED

**1–27**

Pretend that one of Schubert's long-lost relatives has come to you requesting that you write the fourth movement of Symphony No. 8. You realize that this is your big chance to gain world fame in the field of composition. Here's what you'll do. Compose two individual percussion scores to accompany the theme below, which is really the second theme from the first movement. The first measure is done for you.

**Symphony No. 8 ("Unfinished")**
(Fourth Movement)

Play on C melody Instrument

**Franz Schubert and**

______________________

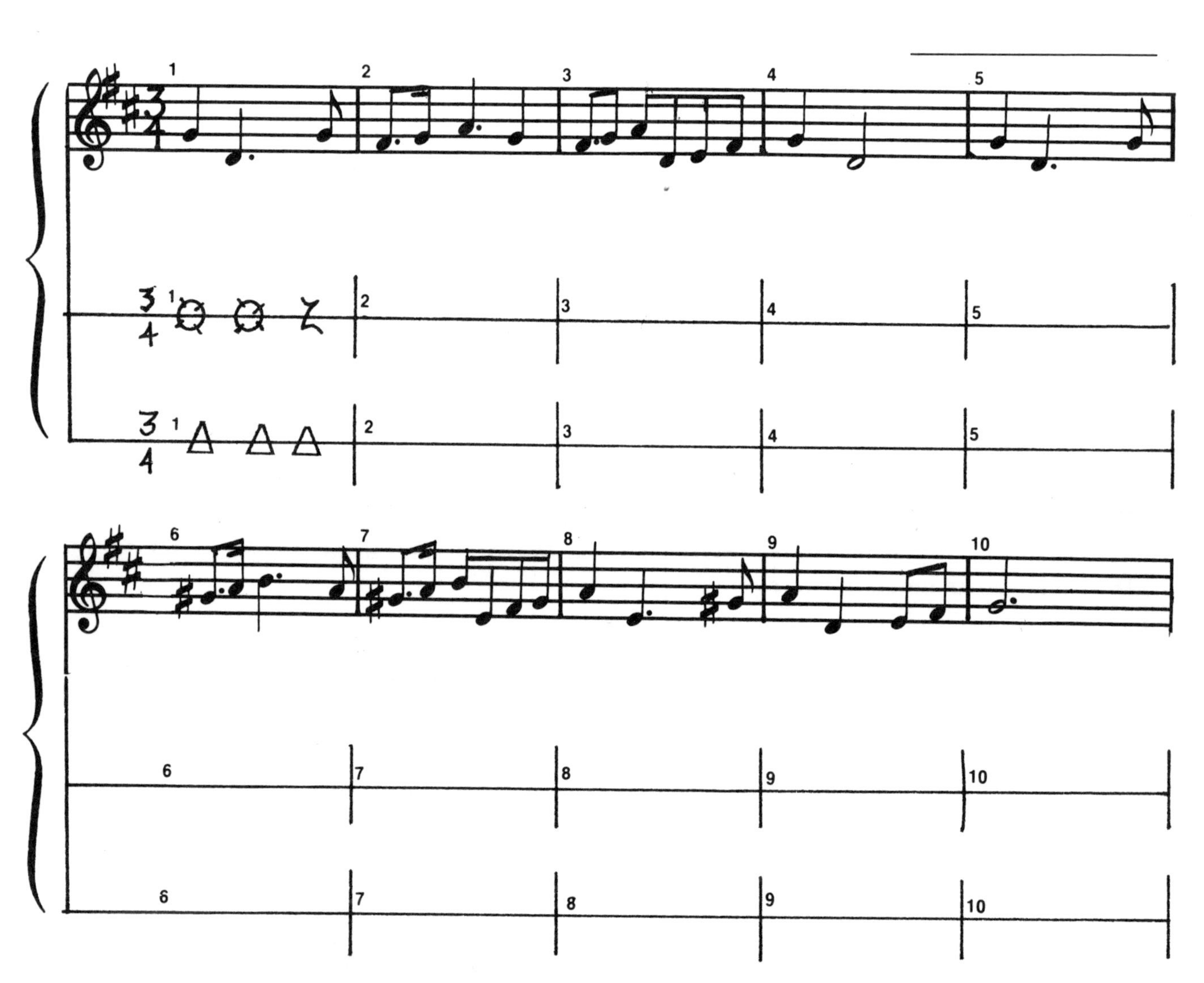


= tambourine    = rest    = triangle

Name ____________________ Score ________

Date ____________________ Class ________

## IT'S ALL YOURS

1–28

The first two measures of this song are complete. Finish composing the tune and give the song a title.

Name ______________________________ Score __________

Date ______________________________ Class __________

## TIE IT UP

1–29

Study the beginning words of these songs below. Then connect the appropriate notes together with ties. A TIE is a curved line that connects two notes of the same pitch. The second note is a continuation of the first and not played separately ( ♩‿♩ , ♩⁀♩ ).

**1. Everybody Loves Saturday Night** **Folk Song**

**2. Cradle Song** **Brahms**

**3. She'll Be Comin' 'Round the Mountain** **Folk Song**

**4. My Bonnie** **Traditional**

**5. Hail! Hail! The Gang's All Here** **Traditional**

**6. Ave Maria** **Franz Schubert**

Name ______________________________ Score __________

Date ______________________________ Class __________

## THE CASE OF THE MISSING DOTS 1–30

In this song the dots from all the dotted notes have been left out. A DOT increases the value of a note by one-half. A dot may be added to any kind of note to increase its value. A dot is added to the right of the note head. For example, 𝅗𝅥. = 3 counts = ( 𝅗𝅥 + ♩ ). Listen to someone play or sing the song, or listen to a recording to hear the correct rhythm. Then add the dots after the right notes.

**Finlandia**

**Jean Sibelius**

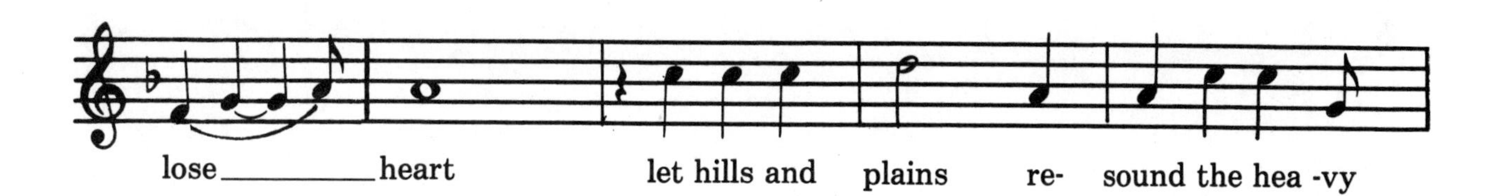

# Activities for Learning
# KEYS AND SCALES

Name ______________________ Score ________

Date ______________________ Class ________

## DIFFER BETWEEN SHARPS AND FLATS



A sharp sign before a note ( or ) means to play the next key to the right. Sharped notes are always higher in pitch than the natural notes with the same letter names.

Draw a sharp before each note.

1.

2.

A flat sign ( or ) before a note means to play the next note to the left. Flatted notes are always lower in pitch than the natural notes with the same letter names.

Draw a flat before each note.

3.

4.

Name ______________________________ Score __________

Date ______________________________ Class __________

## NAME THE KEY SIGNATURE 1–32

Decide the Key Signature of each of the Major Scales. Write the Key Signature on the blank and draw the matching sharps or flats in order on the staff with the Treble Clef sign.

1. Key of ______

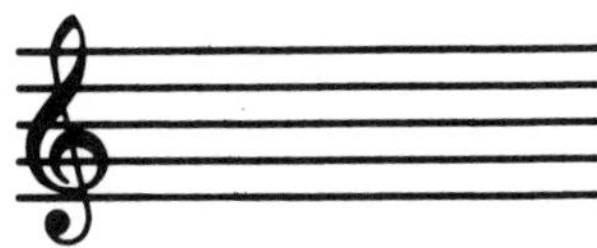

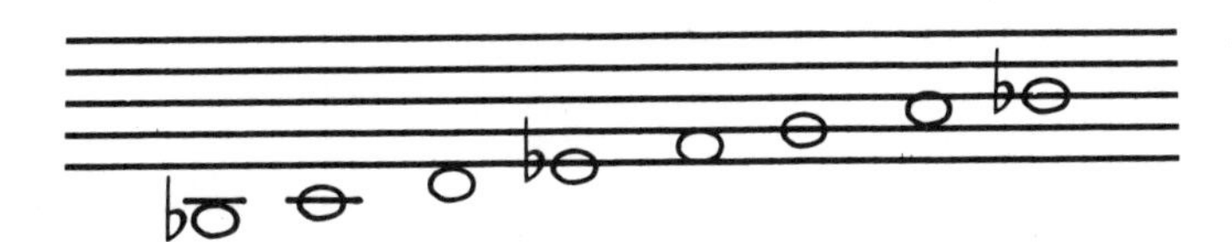

2. Key of ______

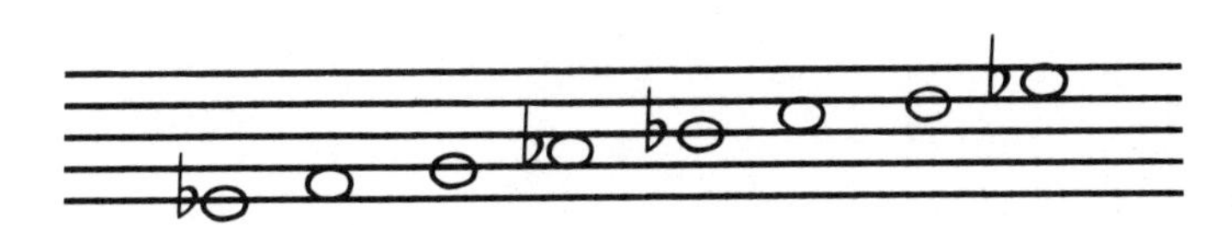

3. Key of ______

4. Key of ______

5. Key of ______

6. Key of ______

Name ______________________________ Score ________

Date ______________________________ Class ________

## HELP THE PERFORMER

**1-33**

Each of these three transcriptions of "Ode to Joy" was copied without the Key Signature. The Key Signatures are shown above the songs. Draw the accidentals ( ♯ and ♭ ) to show the performer the proper notes to play. The first measure is done for you.

### Ode to Joy (from the Ninth Symphony)

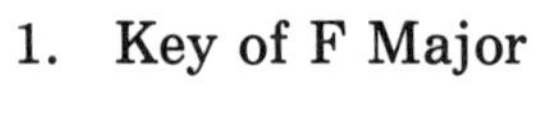

1. Key of F Major

**Beethoven**

2. Key of E♭ Major

3. Key of D Major

Name ______________________________ Score __________

Date ______________________________ Class __________

## CLIMB THE LADDER

1–34

Write the letter names of these Major Scales on the steps of these ladders. Use the example as a guide.

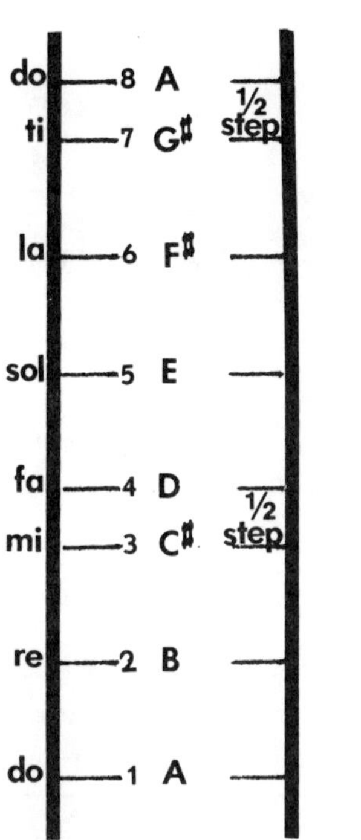


Example: Key of A

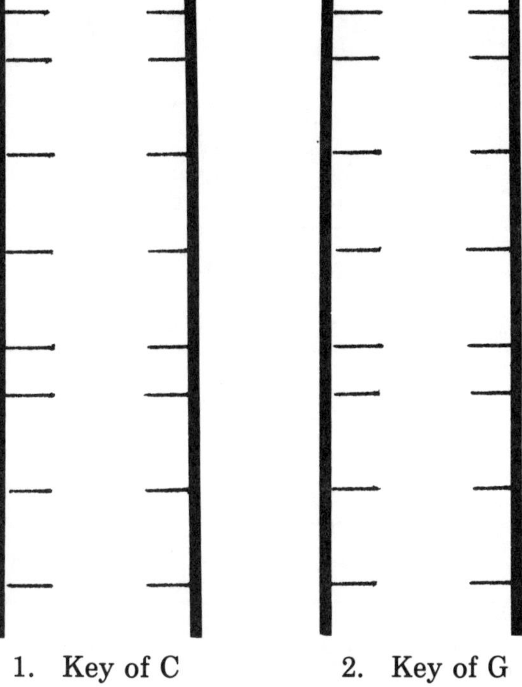

1. Key of C

2. Key of G

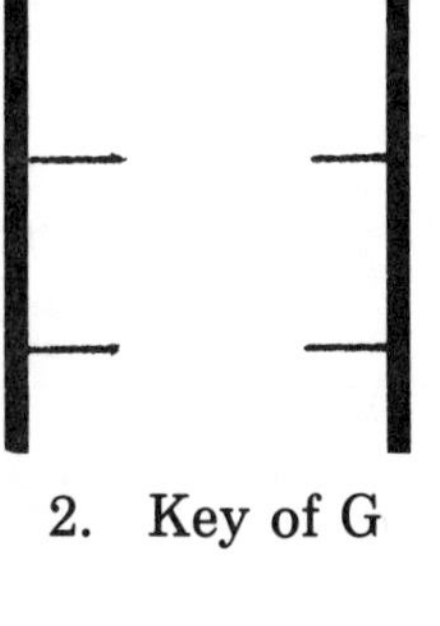

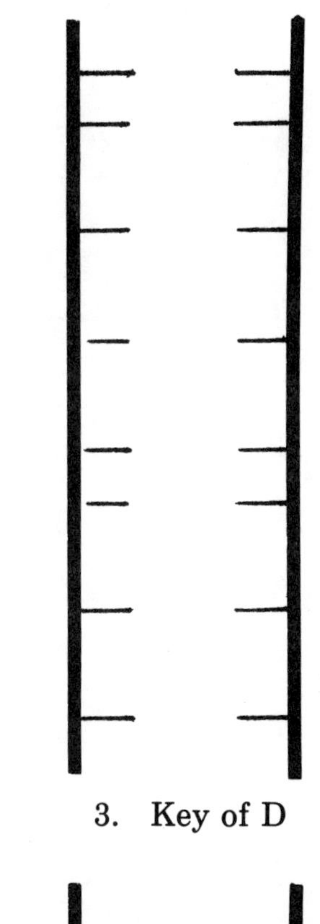

3. Key of D

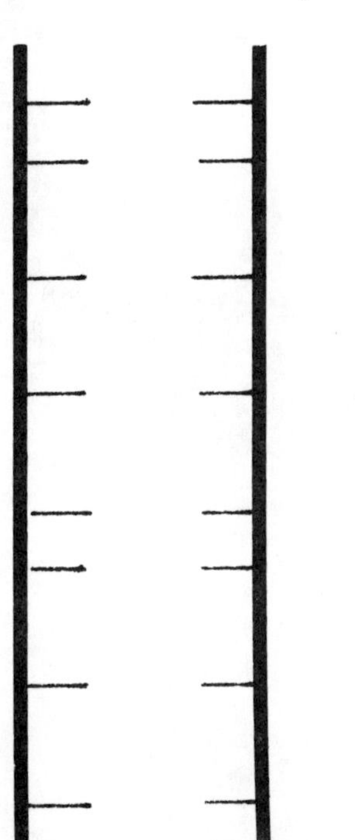

4. Key of F

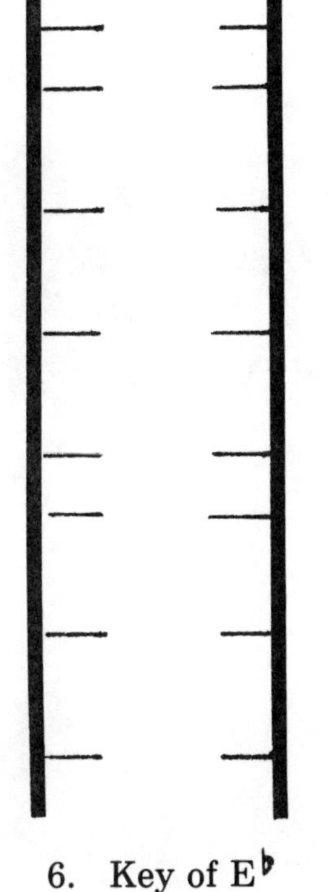

5. Key of B♭

6. Key of E♭

7. Key of A♭

Name ______________________ Score ________

Date ______________________ Class ________

## FIND THE KEYNOTE

1–35

The letter names of the notes for six Major scales are given here, but they do not begin with the Keynote. The first or starting note of a scale is called the KEYNOTE. The Keynote is also referred to as the TONIC. First underline the starting note of the scale and name the Key. Then rewrite the scale beginning with the Keynote on the line below.

A B C D E F♯ G

1. Key of ______ ______________________

A B C♯ D E F♯ G

2. Key of ______ ______________________

A B C D E F G

3. Key of ______ ______________________

A B♭ C D E F G

4. Key of ______ ______________________

A B♭ C D E♭ F G

5. Key of ______ ______________________

A♭ B♭ C D E♭ F G

6. Key of ______ ______________________

Name ______________________ Score ________

Date ______________________ Class ________

## TRANSPOSE HAYDN'S TUNE 1–36

Answer the following about "Haydn's Tune" before transposing it to the Key of F Major.

1. "Haydn's Tune" is written in the Key of ______________________.
2. On what scale degree does the tune begin? ______________________
3. To transpose the tune to the Key of F Major, name the flat in the Key Signature. ________
4. For music written in the Key of F Major, the Keynote is ______________________.
5. The Keynote for the Key of F Major is one scale degree ________ than the Keynote for the Key of G Major.
   higher/lower
6. Begin to transpose "Haydn's Tune" by writing in the Key Signature and Time Signature after the Treble Clef sign. Remember to write the Key Signature on the second staff after the clef sign. The first two notes of the song are already drawn. Finish transposing the tune, then circle the flatted notes throughout the melody.



**Haydn's Tune**

Key of G Major

**Haydn's Tune** (Transposed)

Key of F Major

# Activities for Learning
# TERMINOLOGY

Name ______________________________ Score __________

Date ______________________________ Class __________

## SYMBOLICALLY SPEAKING



Draw the symbols to match their names. Use the answers to the right.

| | | | |
|---|---|---|---|
| 1. WHOLE NOTE | 2. HALF NOTE | 3. QUARTER NOTE | 4. EIGHTH NOTE |
| 5. WHOLE REST | 6. HALF REST | 7. QUARTER REST | 8. EIGHTH REST |
| 9. SHARP | 10. FLAT | 11. NATURAL | 12. METER SIGNATURE |
| 13. STAFF | 14. BAR LINE | 15. TREBLE CLEF | 16. BASS CLEF |
| 17. MEASURE | 18. REPEAT | 19. TIE | 20. SLUR |

Name ______________________ Score ________

Date ______________________ Class ________

## NOTE THE NAMES

1–38

The names of six symbols are given here, but each is incomplete. Find the missing letters by reading the notes. Then write the letters in the blanks. Draw the symbol in the box under the name.

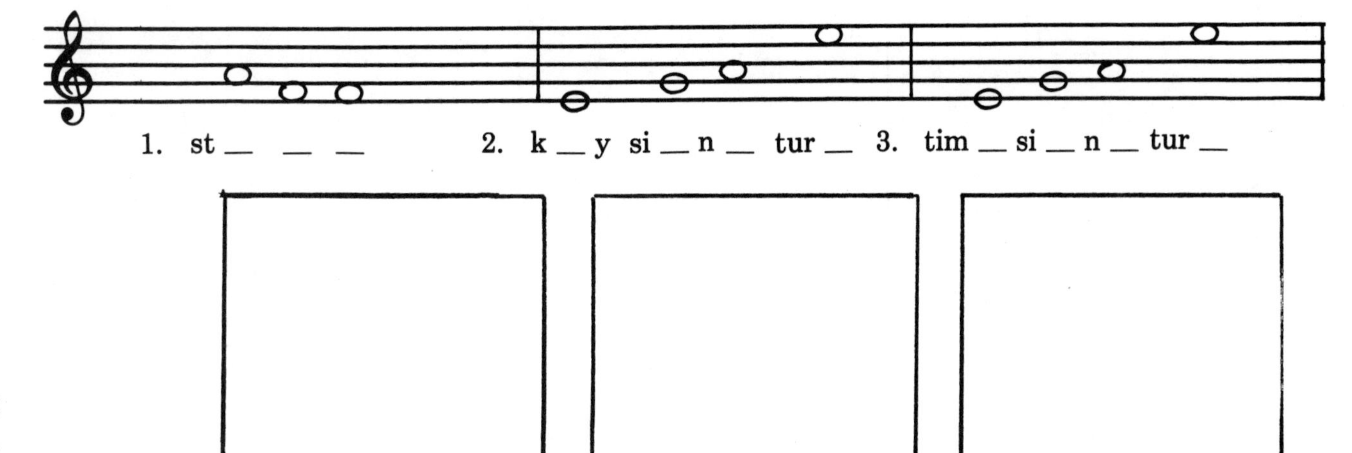


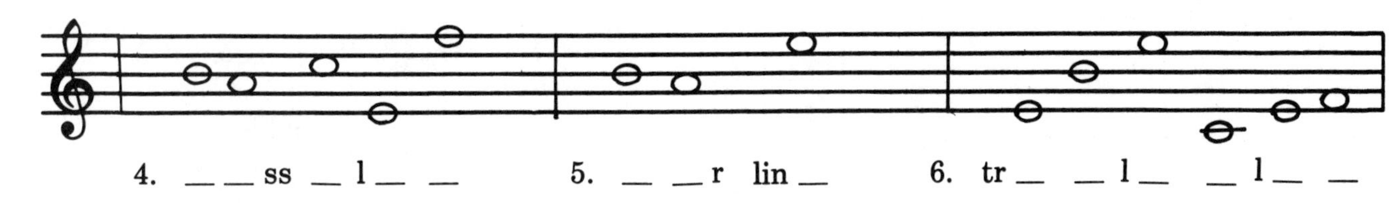

Clues:

Name ______________________ Score ________

Date ______________________ Class ________

## WRITE THE NAMES

**1-39**

Under each symbol write its name. The book cover gives the clues.

| | |
|---|---|
| 1. | 2. |
| 3. | 4. |
| 5. | 6. |
| 7. | 8. |
| 9. | 10. |
| 11. | 12. |

School Assignments

*NOTES & RESTS*

Whole
Half
Quarter
Eighth

*SYMBOLS*

Staff
Treble Clef
Bar Line
Double Bar Line
Sharp
Flat

Name ______________________ Score ________

Date ______________________ Class ________

## MUSIC TALK



Each of these words has two or more meanings. Decide the music meaning and draw the picture to match it.

| | | | |
|---|---|---|---|
| 1. REST | 2. MEASURE | 3. QUARTER | 4. METER |
| 5. STAFF | 6. CLEF | 7. KEY | 8. TIE |
| 9. SHARP | 10. SCALE | 11. ACCIDENTAL | 12. FLAT |

Name ______________________________ Score ________

Date ______________________________ Class ________

## MINI CROSSWORD PUZZLE #1 

Fill in the sentences below with the correct words. Then write them in the puzzle. The words may go either across or down.

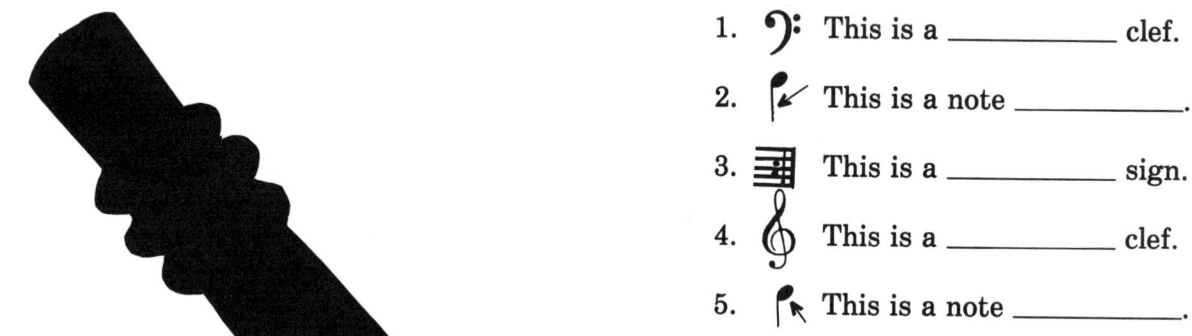

1. This is a __________ clef.
2. This is a note __________.
3. This is a __________ sign.
4. This is a __________ clef.
5. This is a note __________.
6. What instrument is shown here? __________
7. This is a __________ note.

8. This is an __________ note.
9. This is a __________ note.
10. This is a __________ note.

Name ______________________ Score ________

Date ______________________ Class ________

## MINI CROSSWORD PUZZLE #2

1–42

Fill in the sentences below with the correct words. Then write them in the puzzle. The words may go either across or down.

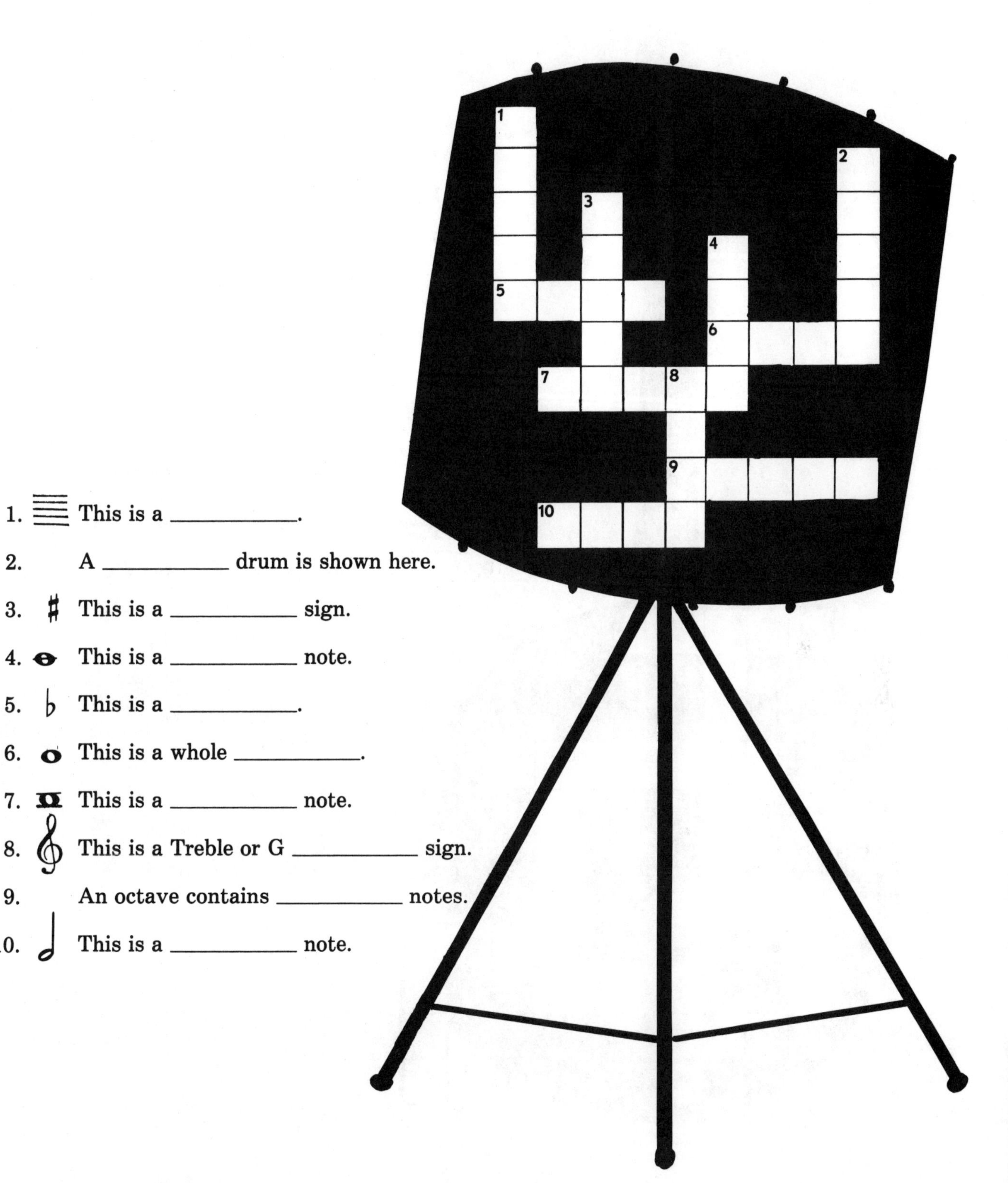

1. This is a ___________.
2. A ___________ drum is shown here.
3. ♯ This is a ___________ sign.
4. This is a ___________ note.
5. ♭ This is a ___________.
6. This is a whole ___________.
7. This is a ___________ note.
8. 𝄞 This is a Treble or G ___________ sign.
9. An octave contains ___________ notes.
10. This is a ___________ note.

Name ______________________________ Score ________

Date ______________________________ Class ________

## MINI CROSSWORD PUZZLE #3 1–43

Fill in the sentences below with the correct words. Then write them in the puzzle. The words may go either across or down.

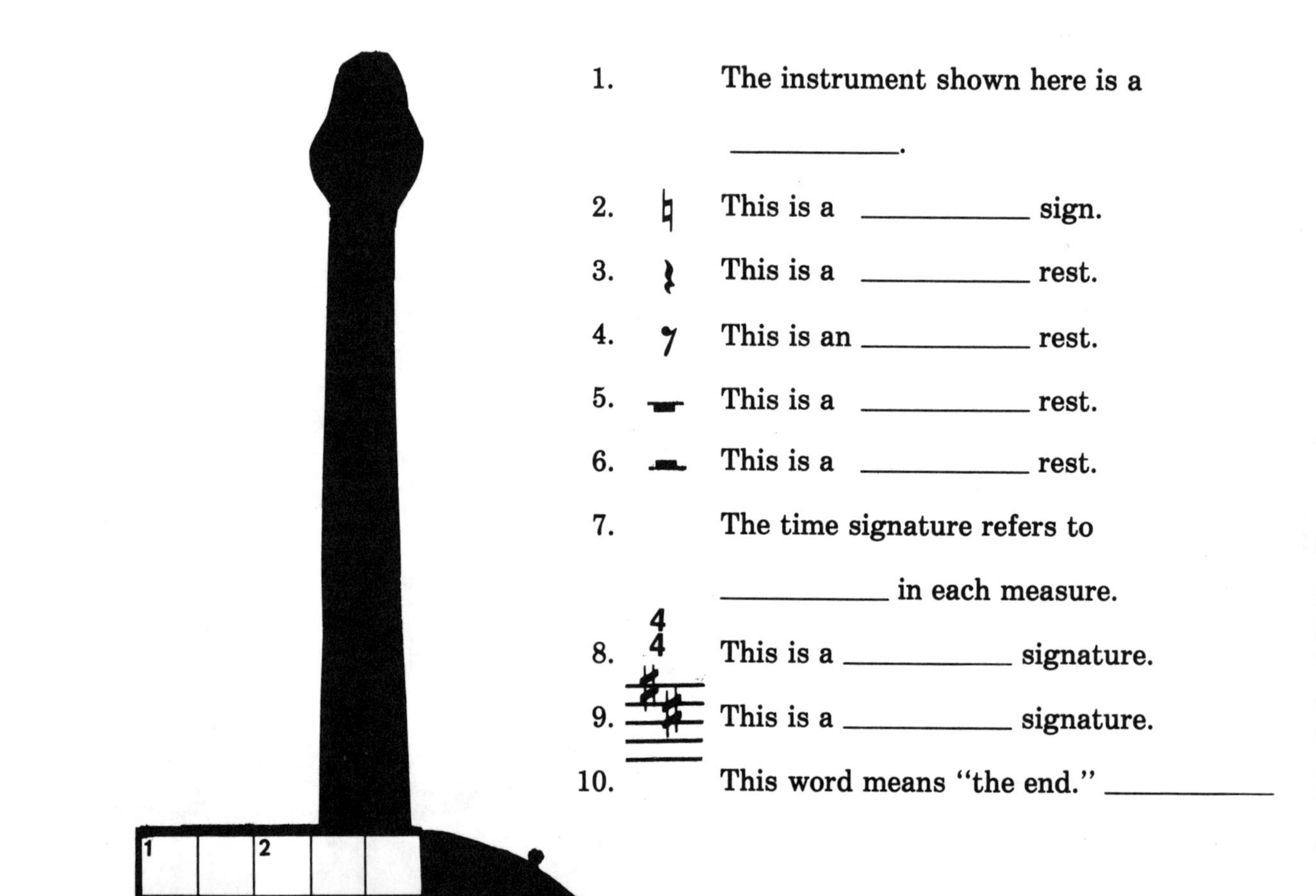

1. The instrument shown here is a ____________.
2. ♮ This is a ____________ sign.
3. 𝄽 This is a ____________ rest.
4. 𝄾 This is an ____________ rest.
5. 𝄻 This is a ____________ rest.
6. 𝄼 This is a ____________ rest.
7. The time signature refers to ____________ in each measure.
8. $\frac{4}{4}$ This is a ____________ signature.
9. ♯♯ This is a ____________ signature.
10. This word means "the end." ____________

Name ______________________ Score ________

Date ______________________ Class ________

## MINI CROSSWORD PUZZLE #4

1–44

Fill in the sentences below with the correct words. Then write them in the puzzle. The words may go either across or down.

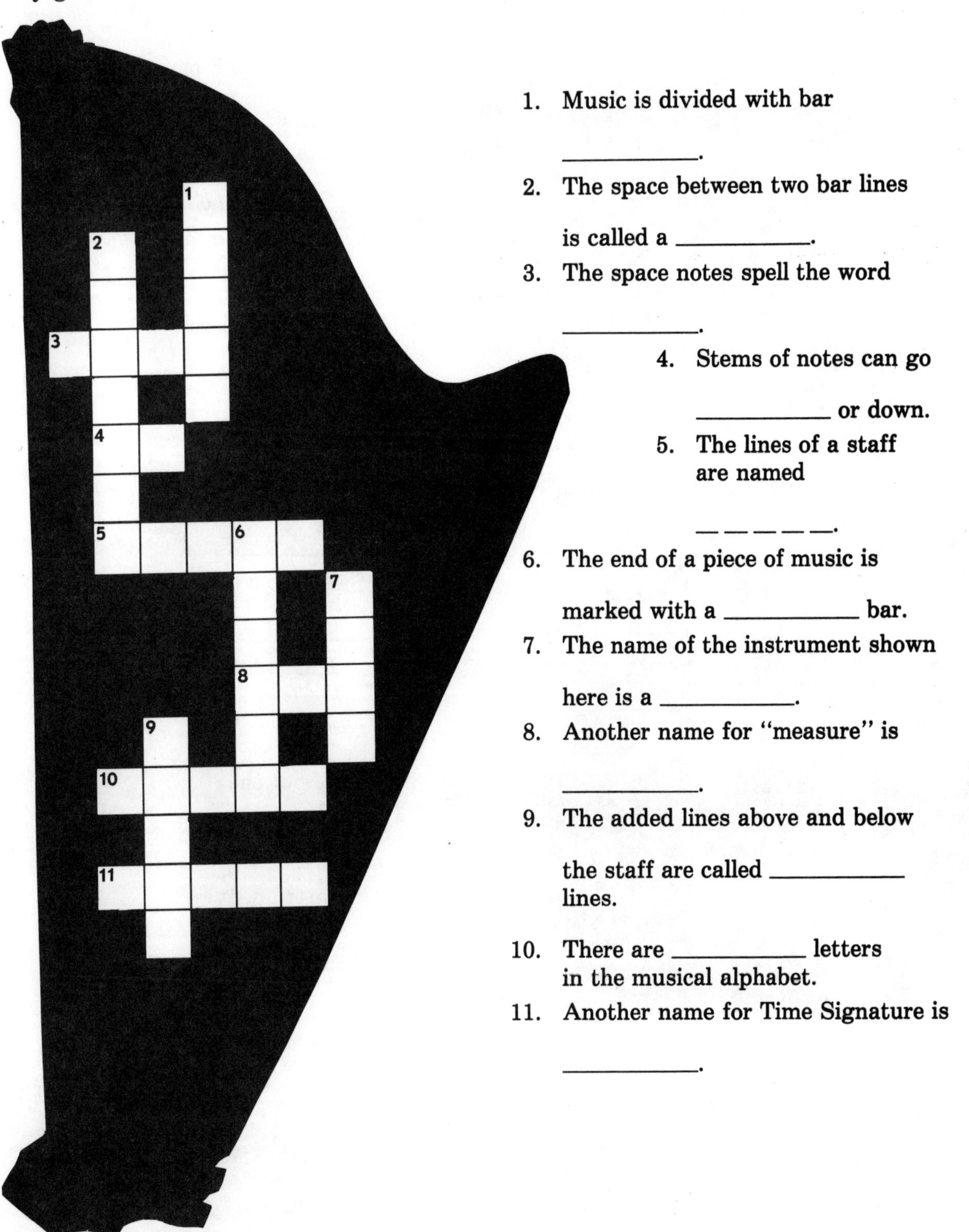


1. Music is divided with bar __________.
2. The space between two bar lines is called a __________.
3. The space notes spell the word __________.
4. Stems of notes can go __________ or down.
5. The lines of a staff are named _ _ _ _ _.
6. The end of a piece of music is marked with a __________ bar.
7. The name of the instrument shown here is a __________.
8. Another name for "measure" is __________.
9. The added lines above and below the staff are called __________ lines.
10. There are __________ letters in the musical alphabet.
11. Another name for Time Signature is __________.

Name ______________________________ Score ________

Date ______________________________ Class ________

## MINI CROSSWORD PUZZLE #5 

Fill in the sentences below with the correct words. Then write them in the puzzle. The words may go either across or down.

1. 𝄢 This is the F or __________ Clef.
2. Major and minor Keys have the __________ key signatures.
3. 𝅘𝅥𝅯 This is a sixteenth __________.
4. C ₵ These are __________ signatures.
5. The note on the first leger line under the treble staff is __________ C.
6. 𝄿 This is a sixteenth __________.
7. 𝄞 This is a G or __________ Clef.
8. The Time Signature tells about the __________ of the music.
9. The instrument shown here is a __________.

Name ______________________ Score ________

Date ______________________ Class ________

## MINI CROSSWORD PUZZLE #6 1–46

Fill in the sentences below with the correct words. Then write them in the puzzle. The words may go either across or down.

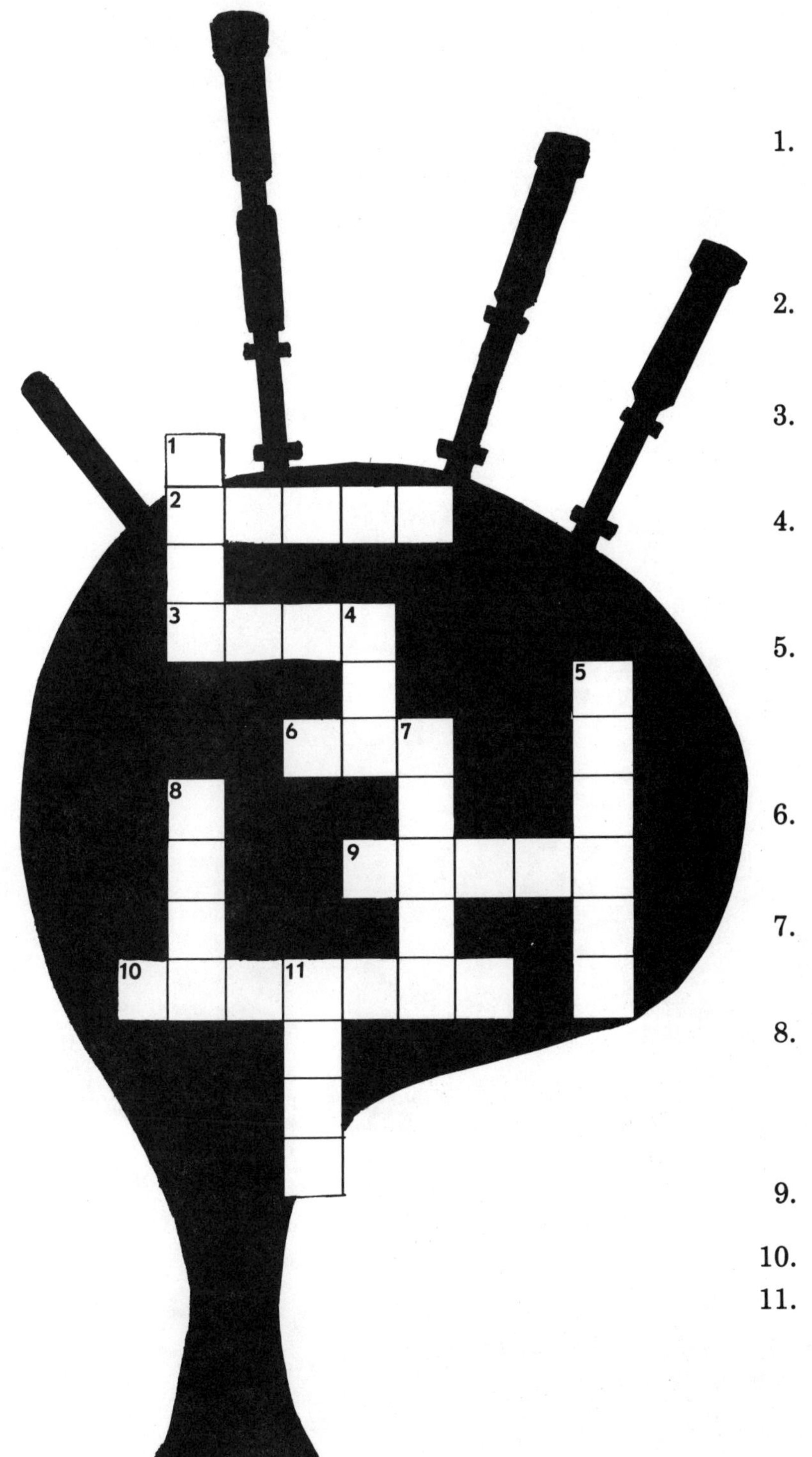


1. A curved line over or under several different notes is a __________.
2. A flat is __________ than a natural note with the same letter name.
3. A silent beat in music is called a __________.
4. Most time signatures consist of __________ numbers.
5. > ∧ ∨ These are __________ marks showing that notes should be played or sung strongly.
6. A small __________ after a note increases its value by one-half.
7. In "waltz" time there are __________ beats to a measure.
8. C This time signature shows that a piece is written in __________ four time.
9. ♪ This is a __________ note.
10. ♩♩♩ (3) This is a __________.
11. The instrument shown here is a bag__________.

Name ____________________ Score ________

Date ____________________ Class ________

# EXPLORING THE UNKNOWN

1–47

Have you ever explored a new area looking at different sights? Pretend you will do that here. Start at "1" and follow the path to the end where you see the bus. Do this by filling in the blocks with the answers to the questions below. The last letter of the first word is the first letter of the next word, and so on.

1. Another name for the Keynote.
2. The sound of two or more notes played or sung together.
3. A piece for two performers.
4. ♩♫
5. A musical sound.
6. ♪ note.
7. 𝅗𝅥 note.
8. 𝄐
9. The lowest voices of women and children.
10. A play or drama set entirely to music.
11. To sing unaccompanied.
12. Very slowly and leisurely (Italian).
13. A woodwind instrument using two reeds.

Name ______________________________ Score ________

Date ______________________________ Class ________

## PUZZLE IN A MAZE 1-48

Have you ever walked through a maze surrounded with bushes? Pretend that you are going to do that now. Start at Number 1, then turn the corner at Number 2 and continue on through Number 16. The trick in going through a maze is not to get lost. Fill in the words suggested by the clues. The last letter of the first word is the first letter of the second word, and so on.

1. The chorus at the end of every stanza in certain songs.
2. A sign that cancels a sharp or flat.
3. An Italian term meaning "smooth."
4. A piece for eight performers.
5. A term meaning "trembling," to rapidly repeat a note.
6. Composers use this word in numbering their pieces. It means "work."
7. The Time _______ indicates the type of meter and the unit of beat.
8. Music listening; two words.
9. "Music" comes from the _______ word "mousikē."
10. The levers moved to make piano action strike the strings.
11. There are _____ letters in the Musical Alphabet.
12. A symbol used to show pitch and duration.
13. Grace notes are added to music for ____.
14. Pertaining to tone.
15. The words of a song.
16. A curved line connecting notes to be sung to the same syllable.

Name ______________________________ Score ________

Date ______________________________ Class ________

## RACE TO THE FINISH 1–49

Race to the middle of this winding path puzzle by filling in the blocks with the words suggested by the clues. The last letter of the first word is the first letter of the next word, and so on. Look at the box of "Scrambled Answers" if you need help.

1. An overtone; pertaining to harmony.
2. A piece with several movements for one or more solo instruments with orchestra.
3. A musical introduction to an opera or oratorio.
4. (Fr.) An audience call for a repeat performance.
5. ♪ = __________ note.
6. 𝅗𝅥 = __________ note.

7. (It.) Meaning "the end."
8. (It.) Meaning "and."

SLOWER TRAFFIC KEEP RIGHT

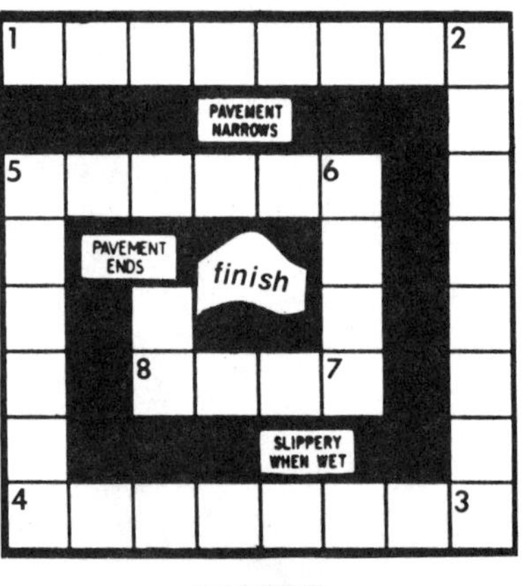


ONE WAY

Draw your dream prize when you're finished.

SCRAMBLED ANSWERS

1. homanric
2. cerconot
3. vuretore
4. conere
5. highet
6. flah
7. nife
8. te

Name ______________________ Score ________

Date ______________________ Class ________

# WANT TO PERFORM?

1-50

Below are signs for the musician to use. The first and last letters for the names of each sign are given. Fill in the missing letters on the blanks to name the signs.

1. > ∧ A _ _ _ _ _ _ s
2. S _ _ _ _ _ _ _ d M _ _ k
3. , B _ _ _ _ h M _ _ k
4. S _ _ _ _ _ _ _ o
5. S _ _ r
6. tr~~~~ T _ _ _ l
7. R _ _ _ _ t S _ _ n
8. T _ e
9. Ped. L _ _ d P _ _ _ l
10. ⊓ D _ _ n B _ w
11. V Up B _ w
12. |%| M _ _ _ _ _ _ e R _ _ _ _ t S _ _ n
13. S _ _ _ f
14. R _ _ _ _ t

# Answer Key
# for *Basic Music Theory*

For students who are just beginning note reading, "Study Guide Strips" have been created as an aid. (Those particular activity sheets suitable for the Guide are indicated with an asterisk after the activity title.) The page is designed to be duplicated and cut into strips. Place these strips in an accessible area to have on hand and ready to use. Prior to distributing any note reading activity, discuss the range of notes to be used for answers.

**1-1 TREBLE KROSS***

Refer to the appropriate study guide strip for checking placement of notes.

B E D E X F A C E
B L M Y E Y Z M D
D E E D Q M U P G
O P M W M C U Z E
C A U B E A D R Y
A B L I L B S E L
F R U N C B Q M P
E W X O T A G E D
I O P C A G E D M
L B A D G E J K S

**1-2 TREBLE PICTURE PUZZLES***

Refer to the appropriate study guide strip for checking placement of notes.

1. FACE
2. BAG
3. EGG
4. BEE
5. CAB
6. ADE
7. CAGE
8. BED

### 1-3 BASS KROSS*

Refer to the appropriate study guide strip for checking placement of notes.

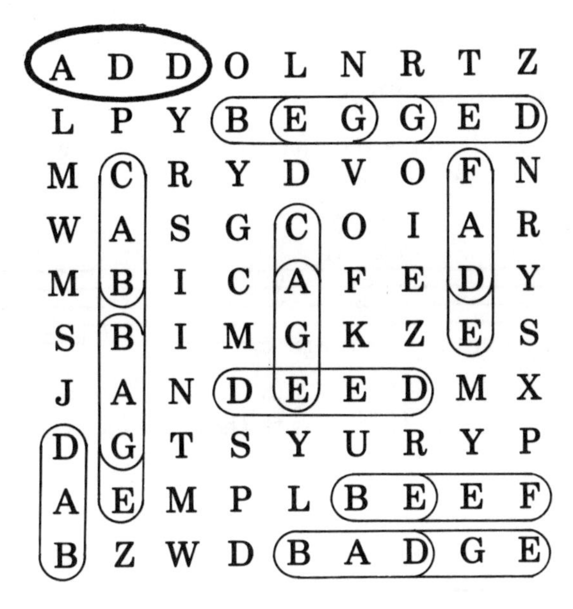


### 1-4 BASS PICTURE PUZZLES*

Refer to the appropriate study guide strip for checking placement of notes.

1. ADD
2. CABBAGE
3. BADGE
4. BED
5. FACE
6. CAB
7. BAGGAGE
8. ACE

### 1-5 KEYS 'N' NOTES*

Refer to the appropriate study guide strip for checking placement of notes.

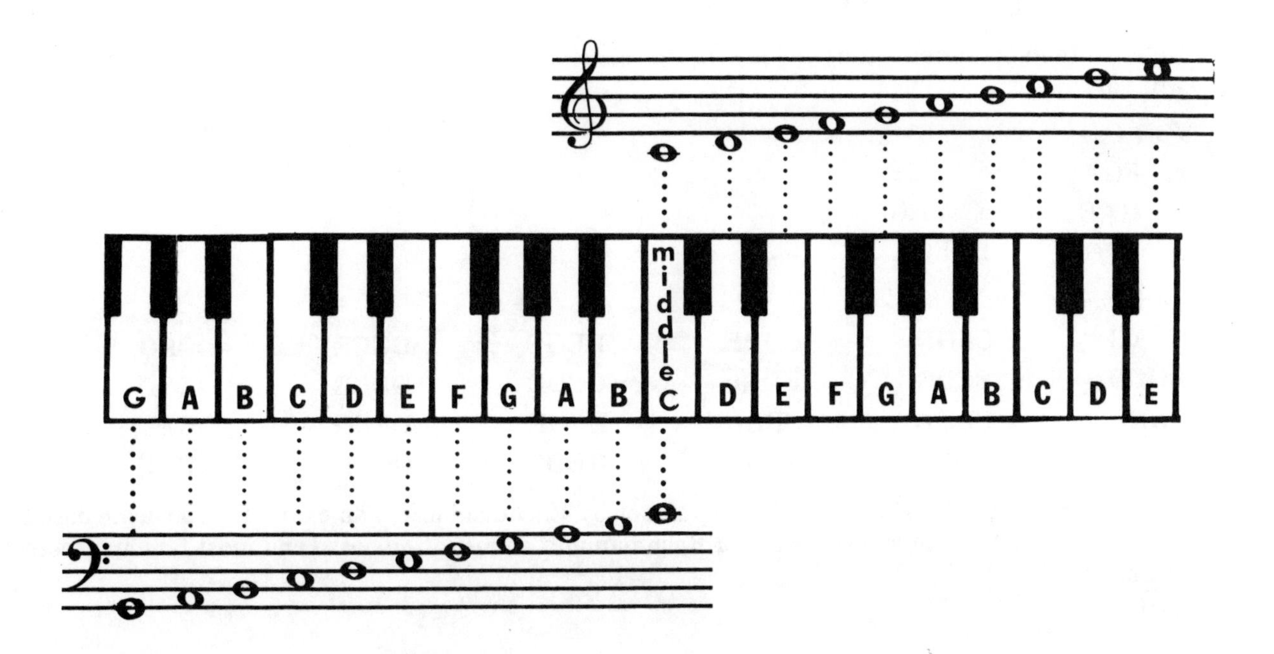

## 1-6 BE ON THE LOOKOUT!

1. a, b
2. b, d
3. e, f
4. b, d, e
5. a, e, f

## 1-7 YOU FIGURE OUT THE DIRECTION*

Refer to the appropriate study guide strip for checking placement of notes.

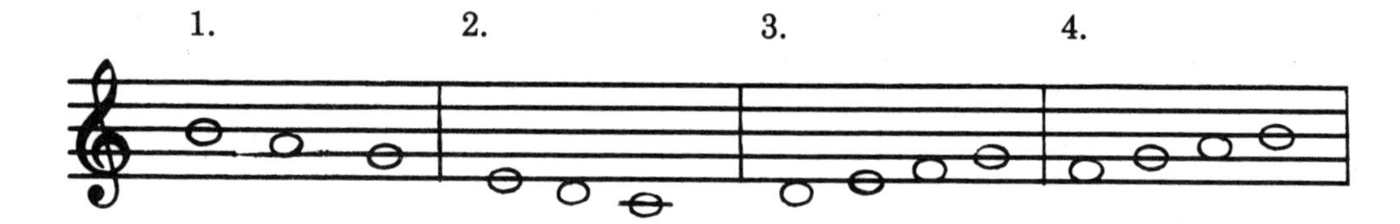


Ask students to draw lines connecting the key with the notes on the staff.

## 1-8 FINISH THE SEQUENCE

## 1-9 REARRANGE THE NOTES*

Refer to the appropriate study guide strip for checking placement of notes. The order of answers will vary.

*Part One*

a. FGA
b. GAF
c. AFG
d. AGF
e. FAG
f. FGA

*Part Two*

| | | | | | |
|---|---|---|---|---|---|
| CDEG | CEGD | CGDE | DEGC | DGCE | DCEG |
| EGCD | ECDG | EDGC | GCDE | GDCE | GECD |
| CGED | CDGE | CEDG | DCGE | DECG | DGEC |
| EDCG | EGDC | ECGD | GEDC | GCED | GDEC |

*Related listening:* The Prelude in C-sharp minor by Rachmaninoff is an example of a theme based on three notes. This piano piece is one of Rachmaninoff's most often heard and most famous pieces of music.

## 1-10 TRANSCRIBE A TUNE

Discuss how many steps higher the notes will be in the Key of C Major than in the Key of A Major. Answer: three steps higher.

Key of C Major

## 1-11 CHORD CLUES

1. Key of C

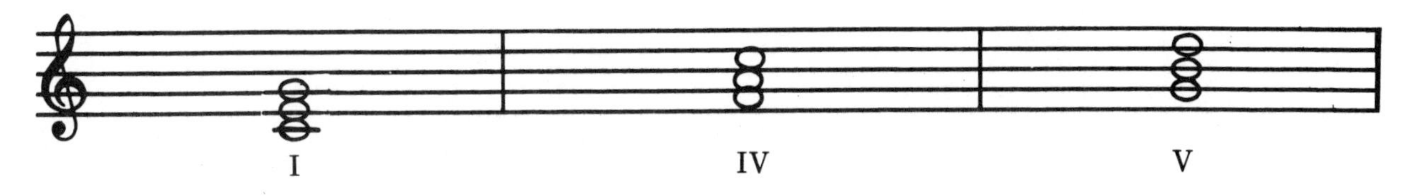

2. Key of F

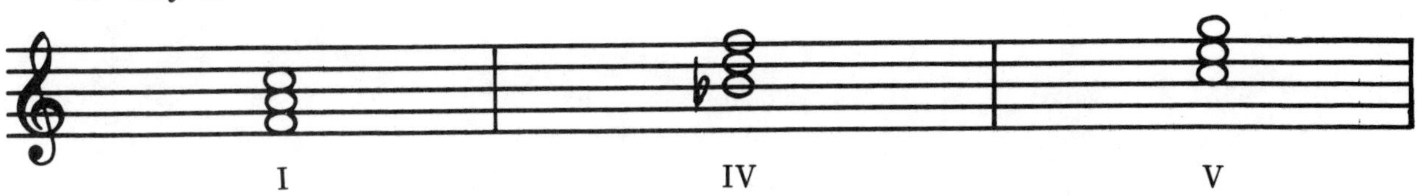


3. Key of G

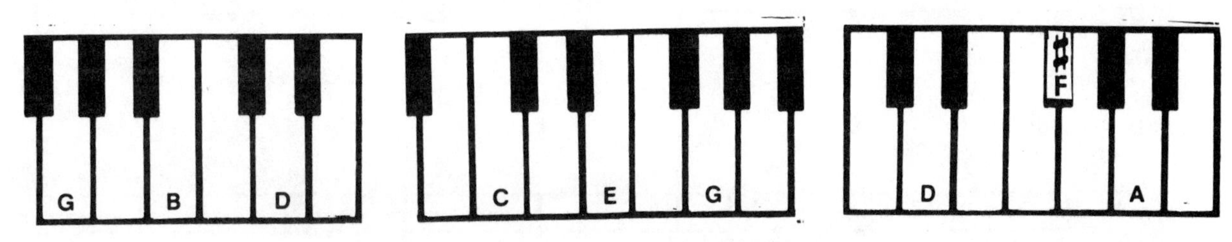

## 1-12 WRITE THE INTERVAL

## 1-13 YOUR MOVE

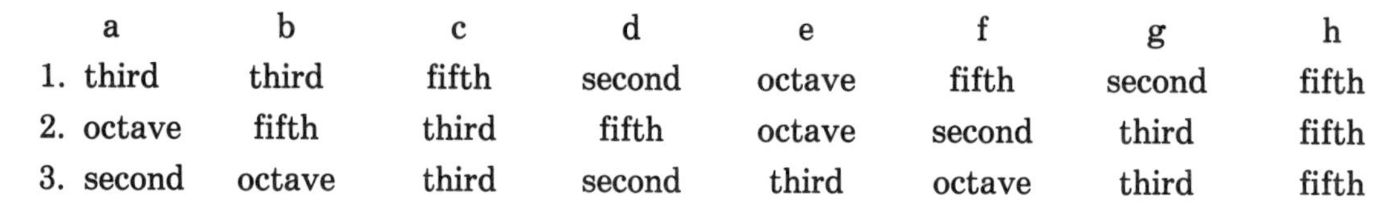

| | a | b | c | d | e | f | g | h |
|---|---|---|---|---|---|---|---|---|
| 1. | third | third | fifth | second | octave | fifth | second | fifth |
| 2. | octave | fifth | third | fifth | octave | second | third | fifth |
| 3. | second | octave | third | second | third | octave | third | fifth |

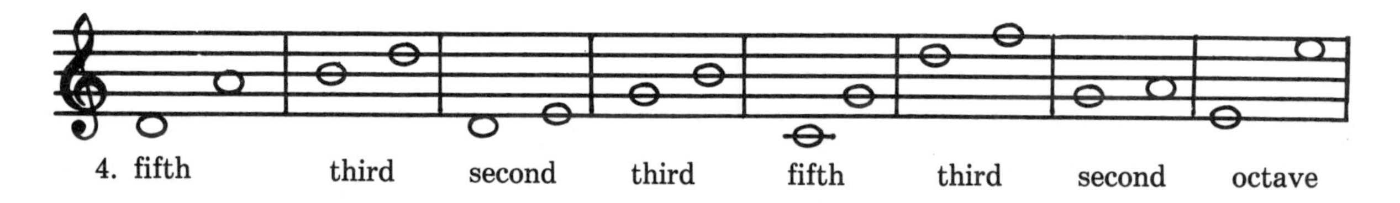


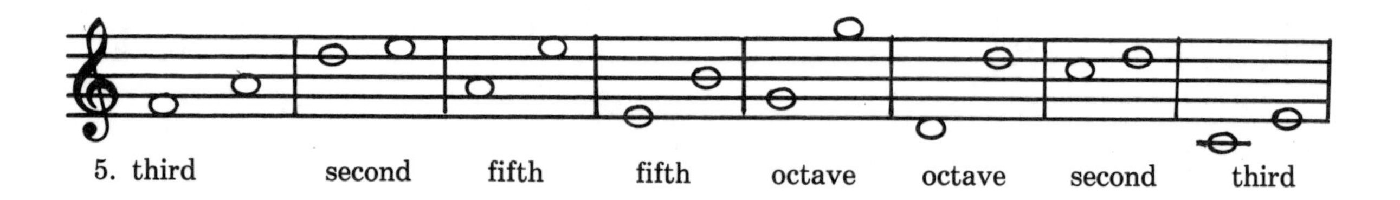

## 1–14 MATCH THE SPEED

Answers will vary.

## 1–15 CLASSIFY THE DYNAMICS

Activity sheet is self-checking.

## 1–16 EXPRESS THE TENSION

Activity sheet is self-checking.

## 1–17 FIND THE LOOK-ALIKES

1. a, e, half
2. a, whole
3. a, b, e, eighth
4. b, d, e, quarter
5. c, half

## 1–18 HELP THE MUSIC MONSTER

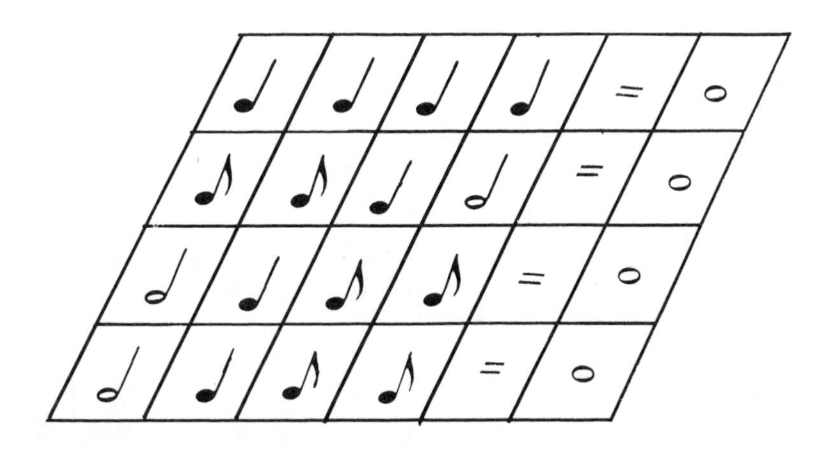

## 1–19 TAKE A REST

1. d, whole
2. a, e, half
3. c, e, quarter
4. b, d, eighth
5. e, sixteenth

## 1–20 COMPUTING RESTS

1. 1
2. 4
3. 2
4. 1
5. ½
6. 2
7. 1
8. 1
9. 1
10. 1
11. 1
12. 2
13. 2
14. 4

## 1-21 MARK THE MEASURES

## 1-22 FINISH THE MEASURES

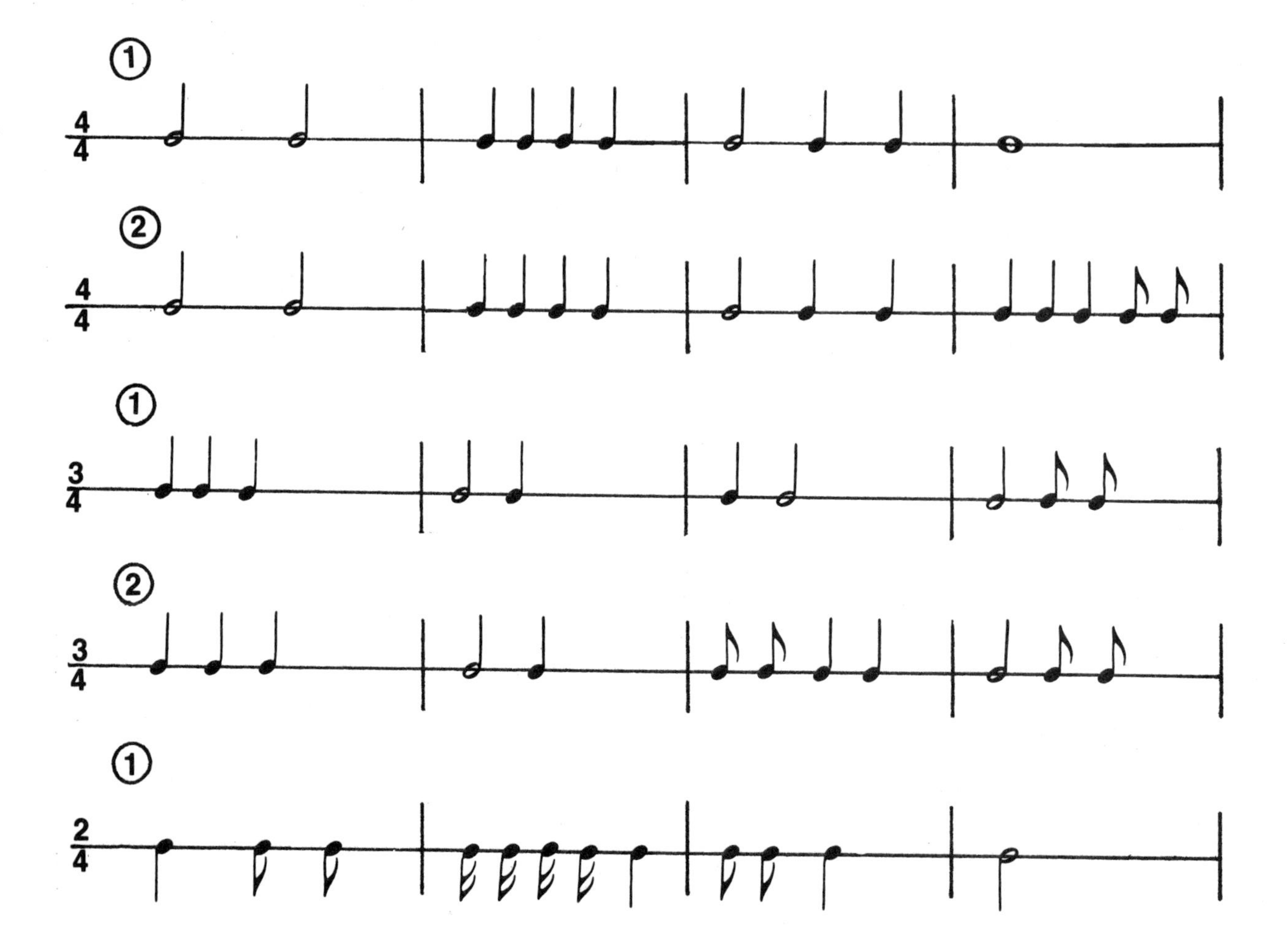

## 1–23 YOU CALL THE TIME

1. $\frac{4}{4}$
2. $\frac{4}{4}$
3. $\frac{3}{4}$
4. $\frac{2}{4}$
5. $\frac{4}{4}$
6. $\frac{2}{4}$
7. $\frac{3}{4}$
8. $\frac{2}{4}$

## 1–24 WRITE THE RHYTHM

Answers will vary.

## 1–25 WHAT'S THE TIME?

Dotted notes ( 𝅗𝅥. ) are included in examples 1 and 5. For beginners, define a "dot" as follows: a dot written after a note lengthens the note by one-half its value. Thus, if 𝅗𝅥 = 2 counts, then 𝅗𝅥. = 3 counts.

"Blow the Man Down" — Traditional Sea Chantey

1. 1 1 1 1 1 1 1 1 1 3 1 1 1 2 1 1 1 1 3

"Lowly Brays the Donkey" — Round

2. 1 1 1 1 2 2 1 1 1 1 4 1 1 1 1 2 2 1 1 1 1 4

"Go Tell Aunt Rhodie" — American Folk Song

3. 2 1 1 2 2 2 1 1 1 1 2 2 1 1 2 1 1 1 1 1 1 4

"Mary Had a Little Lamb" — Traditional

4. 1 1 1 1 1 1 2 1 1 2 1 1 2 1 1 1 1 1 1 2 1 1 1 1 4

"Oh Where Has My Little Dog Gone" — German Song

5. 2 1 1 1 1 1 1 1 2 1 2 1 1 1 1 3 1 1 1

**1–26 COMPOSE AN OSTINATO**

Answers will vary.

**1–27 FINISH THE UNFINISHED**

Answers will vary.

**1–28 IT'S ALL YOURS**

Answers will vary.

**1–29 TIE IT UP**

## 1–30 THE CASE OF THE MISSING DOTS

The rhythm of this song is consistent throughout. Listen for alike measures and phrases. Notice that all half notes are dotted and when a quarter note is placed before an eighth note, it is always dotted.

## 1–31 DIFFER BETWEEN SHARPS AND FLATS

Demonstrate on the keyboard playing sharped notes above the white keys and the flatted notes below the white keys. Each black key can be thought to have both a flat and sharp name. For example: "A sharp" is the same as "B flat," and so on.

## 1–32 NAME THE KEY SIGNATURE

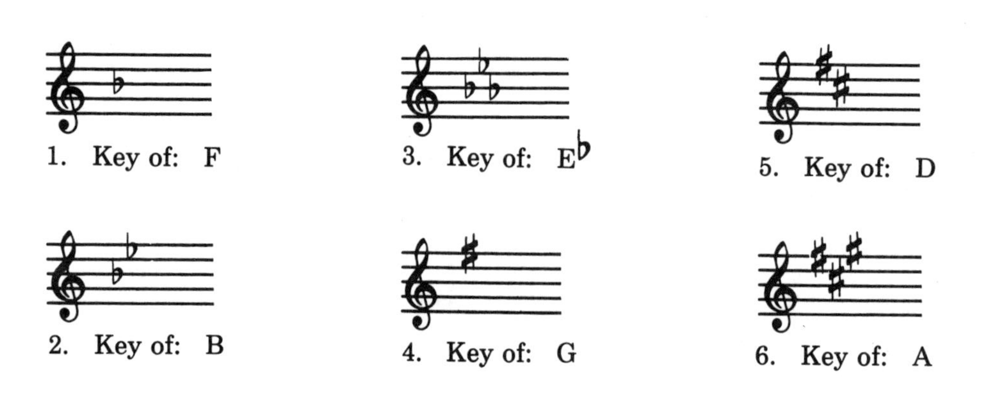


## 1–33 HELP THE PERFORMER

1. Key of F Major

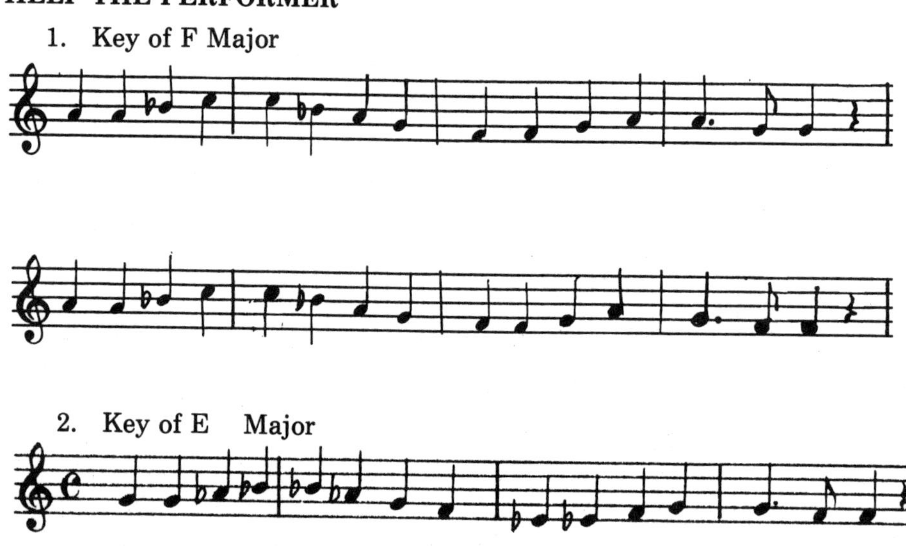

3. Key of D Major

## 1-34 CLIMB THE LADDER

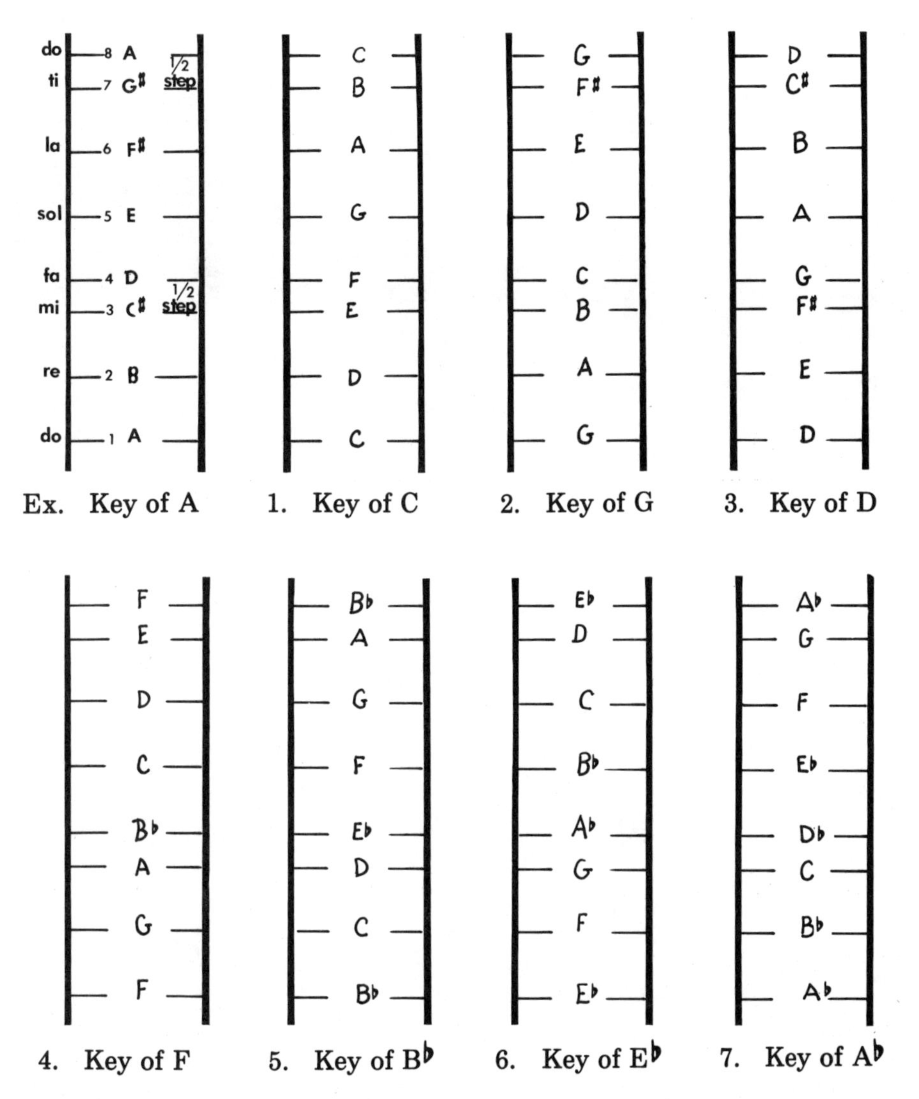


Ex. Key of A 1. Key of C 2. Key of G 3. Key of D

4. Key of F 5. Key of B♭ 6. Key of E♭ 7. Key of A♭

Students should note that the scales all have the same pattern of whole steps and half steps. The half steps always occur between scale degrees 3 and 4, and 7 and 8. When you play any scale on the keyboard, you will have the same sequence of whole steps and half steps.

## 1-35 FIND THE KEYNOTE

| | | | | | | | |
|---|---|---|---|---|---|---|---|
| 1. Key of __G__ (Major) | G | A | B | C | D | E | F♯ |
| 2. Key of __D__ (Major) | D | E | F♯ | G | A | B | C♯ |
| 3. Key of __C__ (Major) | C | D | E | F | G | A | B |
| 4. Key of __F__ (Major) | F | G | A | B♭ | C | D | E |
| 5. Key of __B♭__ (Major) | B♭ | C | D | E♭ | F | G | A |
| 6. Key of __E♭__ (Major) | E♭ | F | G | A♭ | B♭ | C | D |

## 1–36 TRANSPOSE HAYDN'S TUNE

Review stem direction. If a note is placed around the third line, the stem may go in either direction. When a note is placed higher than the third line, the stem will go downward on the left side of the note head.

1. G Major
2. fifth
3. B flat
4. F
5. lower

6\.

## 1–37 SYMBOLICALLY SPEAKING

1.

2.

3.

4.

5.

6.

7.

8.

9.

10.

11.

12.

13.

14.

15.

16.

17.

18.

19.

20.

## 1–38 NOTE THE NAMES

1. staff

2. key signature

3. time signature

4. bass clef

5. bar line

6. treble clef

## 1–39 WRITE THE NAMES

1. double bar line
2. treble clef
3. whole note
4. bar line
5. sharp
6. eighth note
7. half note
8. staff
9. quarter note
10. flat
11. quarter rest
12. half rest

## 1–40 MUSIC TALK

1. 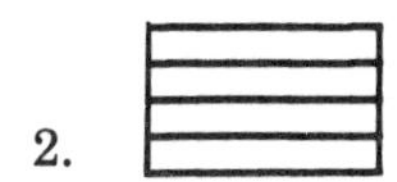


2.

3.

4. 4/4

5. 

6. or

7.

8.

9.

10. 

11.

12.

## 1–41 MINI CROSSWORD PUZZLE #1

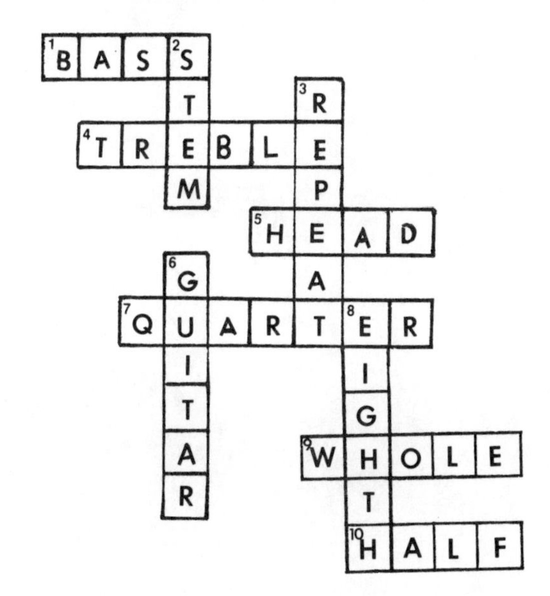

## 1–42 MINI CROSSWORD PUZZLE #2

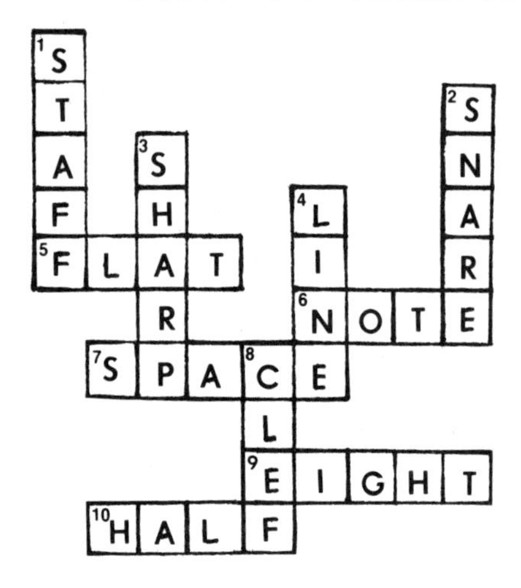


## 1–43 MINI CROSSWORD PUZZLE #3

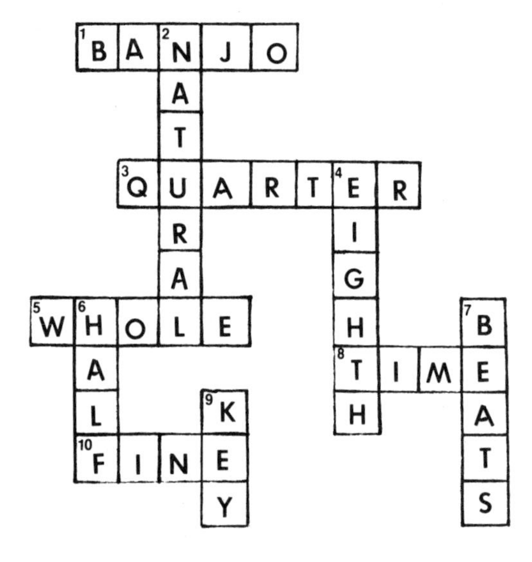


## 1–44 MINI CROSSWORD PUZZLE #4

## 1-45 MINI CROSSWORD PUZZLE #5

| | | | | | | |
|---|---|---|---|---|---|---|
| | | | 1 B | A | 2 S | S |
| | | 3 N | | | A | |
| | | O | | | M | |
| | | 4 T | I | 5 M | E | |
| 6 R | | E | | I | | |
| E | | | | D | | |
| S | | | | D | | |
| 7 T | 8 R | E | B | L | E | |
| | H | | | E | | |
| | Y | | | | | |
| | 9 T | U | B | A | | |
| | H | | | | | |
| | M | | | | | |

## 1-46 MINI CROSSWORD PUZZLE #6

## 1-47 EXPLORING THE UNKNOWN

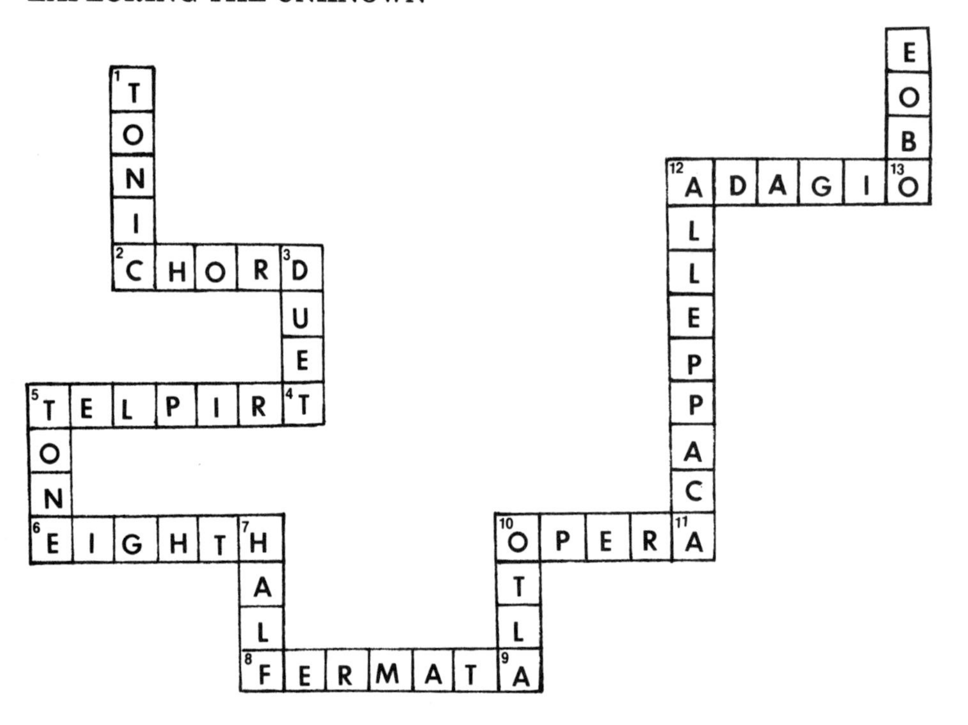


## 1-48 PUZZLE IN A MAZE

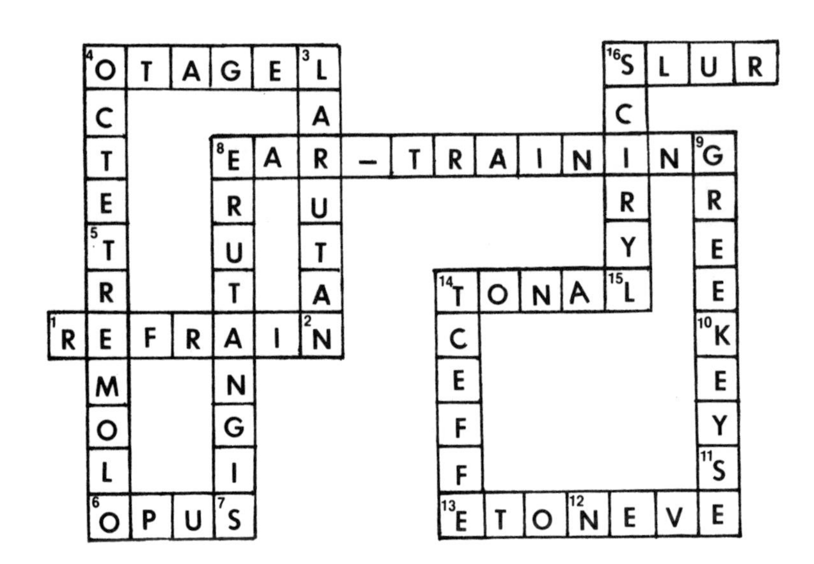

## 1–49 RACE TO THE FINISH

| | | | | | | | |
|---|---|---|---|---|---|---|---|
| 1 H | A | R | M | O | N | I | 2 C |
| | | | | | | | O |
| 5 E | I | G | H | T | 6 H | | N |
| R | | | | | A | | C |
| O | | T | | | L | | E |
| C | | 8 E | N | I | 7 F | | R |
| N | | | | | | | T |
| 4 E | R | U | T | R | E | V | 3 O |

## 1–50 WANT TO PERFORM?

1. Accents
2. Stressed Mark
3. Breath Mark
4. Staccato
5. Slur
6. Trill
7. Repeat Sign
8. Tie
9. Loud Pedal
10. Down Bow
11. Up Bow
12. Measure Repeat Sign
13. Staff
14. Repeat

# Study Guide Strips

Photocopy as many pages as needed. Then cut apart along the dotted lines. Store in easy accessible 3″ × 5″ file box.

Use these "Study Guide Strips" as:

- an aid in completing activities
- as a device for self-checking
- as a pocket study guide for reviewing and studying notes

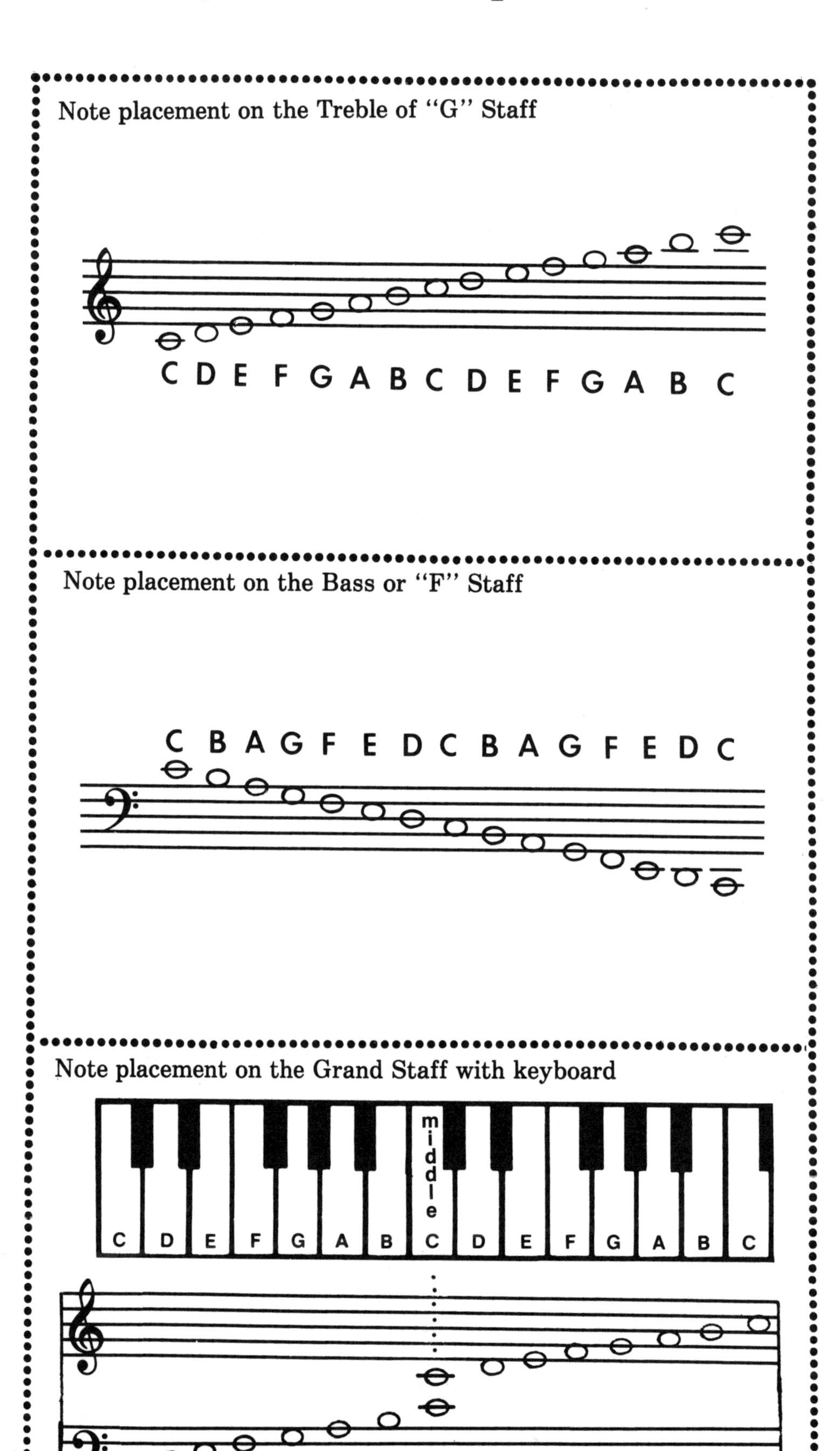

# Progress Chart
# for *Basic Music Theory*

Use this chart to keep a record of activities completed for each class. List your classes (or students) in the given spaces at the right. As each activity is completed for a class, mark an "X" in the appropriate column.

| Activity Number/Title | | Skill Involved | | | | |
|---|---|---|---|---|---|---|
| **Pitch** | | | | | | |
| 1-1 | TREBLE KROSS | Naming notes on the Treble Staff | | | | |
| 1-2 | TREBLE PICTURE PUZZLES | Writing notes on the Treble Staff | | | | |
| 1-3 | BASS KROSS | Naming notes on the Bass Staff | | | | |
| 1-4 | BASS PICTURE PUZZLES | Writing notes on the Bass Staff | | | | |
| 1-5 | KEYS 'N' NOTES | Figuring notation for pitch on the Grand Staff | | | | |
| 1-6 | BE ON THE LOOKOUT! | Locating repeated notes | | | | |
| 1-7 | YOU FIGURE OUT THE DIRECTION | Deciding which direction keys should be played and notating on the staff | | | | |
| 1-8 | FINISH THE SEQUENCE | Completing a progression of notes to finish the sequence | | | | |
| 1-9 | REARRANGE THE NOTES | Rearranging a set of notes on the staff | | | | |
| 1-10 | TRANSCRIBE A TUNE | Transposing a tune with leger lines | | | | |
| 1-11 | CHORD CLUES | Naming and writing chords on the Treble Staff | | | | |
| **Intervals** | | | | | | |
| 1-12 | WRITE THE INTERVAL | Drawing notes and writing letter names of notes to match intervals | | | | |
| 1-13 | YOUR MOVE | Naming seconds, thirds, fifths, and octaves | | | | |

| Activity Number/Title | | Skill Involved | | | | |
|---|---|---|---|---|---|---|
| **Dynamics** | | | | | | |
| 1–14 | MATCH THE SPEED | Drawing stick men to match tempo markings and definitions | | | | |
| 1–15 | CLASSIFY THE DYNAMICS | Classifying dynamic levels by rewriting symbols and names | | | | |
| 1–16 | EXPRESS THE TENSION | Classifying dynamic markings by rewriting symbols and names | | | | |
| **Duration** | | | | | | |
| 1–17 | FIND THE LOOK-ALIKES | Identifying eighth, quarter, half, and whole notes | | | | |
| 1–18 | HELP THE MUSIC MONSTER | Figuring note values of eighth, quarter, half, and whole notes using the note key | | | | |
| 1–19 | TAKE A REST | Matching rests with notes of the same time value | | | | |
| 1–20 | COMPUTING RESTS | Reviewing facts about rests | | | | |
| 1–21 | MARK THE MEASURES | Dividing notes into measures according to time signatures | | | | |
| 1–22 | FINISH THE MEASURES | Looking at time signatures to add a note in the measure | | | | |
| 1–23 | YOU CALL THE TIME | Adding the correct meter signature to match measures | | | | |
| 1–24 | WRITE THE RHYTHM | Composing various rhythms | | | | |
| 1–25 | WHAT'S THE TIME? | Writing appropriate meter signatures to match measures | | | | |
| 1–26 | COMPOSE AN OSTINATO | Composing an ostinato for a percussion instrument for "Are You Sleeping?" | | | | |
| 1–27 | FINISH THE UNFINISHED | Writing two percussion scores | | | | |
| 1–28 | IT'S ALL YOURS | Finish composing a tune and giving it a title | | | | |
| 1–29 | TIE IT UP | Adding ties to notes in familiar song beginnings | | | | |
| 1–30 | THE CASE OF THE MISSING DOTS | Adding dots to notes in "Finlandia" | | | | |
| **Keys and Scales** | | | | | | |
| 1–31 | DIFFER BETWEEN SHARPS AND FLATS | Drawing sharps and flats | | | | |

| Activity Number/Title | | Skill Involved | | | | |
|---|---|---|---|---|---|---|
| 1–32 | NAME THE KEY SIGNATURE | Supplying sharps or flats and naming the key signature | | | | |
| 1–33 | HELP THE PERFORMER | Drawing accidentals for three different key signatures | | | | |
| 1–34 | CLIMB THE LADDER | Writing major scales using letter names | | | | |
| 1–35 | FIND THE KEYNOTE | Identifying the keynote and rewriting the scale | | | | |
| 1–36 | TRANSPOSE HAYDN'S TUNE | Transposing a melody and analyzing it | | | | |

**Terminology**

| | | | | | | |
|---|---|---|---|---|---|---|
| 1–37 | SYMBOLICALLY SPEAKING | Drawing symbols to match names | | | | |
| 1–38 | NOTE THE NAMES | Drawing symbols and writing names using notation | | | | |
| 1–39 | WRITE THE NAMES | Matching names with symbols | | | | |
| 1–40 | MUSIC TALK | Deciding music meanings of words and drawing the symbol | | | | |
| 1–41 | MINI CROSSWORD PUZZLE #1 | Reviewing music terms | | | | |
| 1–42 | MINI CROSSWORD PUZZLE #2 | Reviewing music terms | | | | |
| 1–43 | MINI CROSSWORD PUZZLE #3 | Reviewing music terms | | | | |
| 1–44 | MINI CROSSWORD PUZZLE #4 | Reviewing music terms | | | | |
| 1–45 | MINI CROSSWORD PUZZLE #5 | Reviewing music terms | | | | |
| 1–46 | MINI CROSSWORD PUZZLE #6 | Reviewing music terms | | | | |
| 1–47 | EXPLORING THE UNKNOWN | Reviewing music terminology | | | | |
| 1–48 | PUZZLE IN A MAZE | Reviewing music terminology | | | | |
| 1–49 | RACE TO THE FINISH | Learning terminology | | | | |
| 1–50 | WANT TO PERFORM? | Identifying performance signs | | | | |

# Basic Music Theory

accidental
analyze
bar line
bass clef
bass staff
chord
composing
composition
dotted note
dynamics
eighth note
Fine
flat
half note
interval
keynote
key signature
leger line
major
measure
meter signature
minor
natural
note
octave
ostinato
pitch
quarter note
repeat
rest
rhythm
scale
score
sequence
sharp
sixteenth note
slur
staff
tempo
tie
time signature
transpose
treble clef
treble staff
whole note

Name ______________________________

Date ______________________________

# Craft Project for *Basic Music Theory*

## MINI MUSIC FLASH CARDS

**Objective:** The Mini Music Flash Cards are designed to be an enrichment activity not only for this unit, but for the entire *Library.* They may be used by individual students as a study aid, by two or more students as a drill, or by the entire class as a learning tool in a game. Ideal storage for the Mini Music Flash Cards is the envelope constructed in the craft project for Unit 6, *Special Days Throughout the Year.*

**Materials Needed:**

- Copies of the sheet of flash cards
- Scissors
- Pencil or marker
- *Optional:* Colored construction paper
- *Optional:* Paste

**Construction Directions:**

1. Cut around the outside edge of the sheet of flash cards.
2. You may want to cover the back of the sheet with paste and mount the sheet on a piece of construction paper.
3. When the paste has dried, cut the flash cards apart along the dotted lines.
4. Depending on how you use the flash cards, you might want to write the name of the symbol on the back of each card.

**Uses:** With these Mini Music Flash Cards, students will enjoy learning the names of music symbols and recognizing the signs. You can devise many exciting games that teach students to understand music theory. Here are three to get you started.

## Match 'Em Up

Players use a sheet of 8½" × 11" paper to trace along the dotted lines of the flash cards sheet (before the students cut out the cards) *OR* the paper can be divided by evenly drawing six boxes by four boxes to make 24 blocks. Players then write the names of all the music symbols, as listed below, in order, one name in each block. The object of the game is to match the symbol with the name by placing the flash card on top of the block with the correct name.

The card names from left to right, beginning with the first row, are:

1. treble clef, bass clef, bar line, staff, measure, double bar
2. repeat, Time Signature, whole note, half note, quarter note, eighth note
3. Piano, Forte, whole rest, half rest, quarter rest, eighth rest
4. flat, sharp, natural, Fermata (hold), tie, slur

## Quick Draw

Players lay the cards out with the symbol side up. The leader names a symbol. The first player to hold the correct mini flash card up (chest high) is the winner. That player then becomes the leader, and the game continues.

## Find the Group

Players separate the cards and lay them out in categories and identify the symbols as follows:

Pitch: bass clef, treble clef, flat, sharp, natural

Duration: eighth note, quarter note, half note, whole note, eighth rest, quarter rest, half rest, whole rest

Dynamics: Forte, Piano

Rhythmic: Meter Signature, Fermata (hold)

Performance: hold, slur, bar line, staff, measure, double bar, repeat

Name ______________________________

Date ______________________________

# Incentive Badges

*To the teacher:* Cut apart badges and keep in a handy 3″ × 5″ file box along with tape. Encourage students to write their names and the date on the backs of their badges and to wear them.

**WITH THIS COUPON . . .**

NAME ______________________

IS ENTITLED TO ______________________

______________________

______________________

MUSIC AWARD

For hopping to it!

Good helper badge

in music class.

# MUSIC SHARE-A-GRAM

TO: ______________________________ DATE ____________
(Parent's Name)

FROM: ______________________________ SCHOOL ____________
(Classroom Music Teacher)

RE: ______________________________ CLASS ____________
(Student's Name)

To help you recognize your child's success in music class or any area that needs attention the following observation(s) has/have been made.

| | Exceptional | Satisfactory | Unsatisfactory |
|---|---|---|---|
| Shows musical aptitude | | | |
| Shows creativity | | | |
| Shows talent | | | |
| Shows initiative | | | |
| Self-concept in music class | | | |
| Fairness in dealing with classmates | | | |
| Self-direction | | | |
| Care of instrument and equipment | | | |
| Reaction to constructive criticism | | | |
| Observes music class rules | | | |
| Starts and completes work on time | | | |
| Generally follows directions | | | |

over for comments ►



# RETURN-A-GRAM

TO: ______________________________ DATE ____________
(Classroom Music Teacher)

FROM: ______________________________ SCHOOL ____________
(Parent's Name)

RE: ______________________________ CLASS ____________
(Student's Name)

Please write your comments or questions on the back and return. If you want to be called for a parent-teacher conference, indicate below.

________________________ Class __________ Year __________

(Student's Name)

# STUDENT RECORD PROFILE CHART

Select the appropriate data in parentheses for each category, i, ii, iii, and iv, and record the information in the chart below as shown in the example.

i.—Unit Number for *Music Curriculum Activities Library* (1, 2, 3, 4, 5, 6, 7)

ii.—Date (Day/Month)

iii.—Semester (1, 2, 3, 4) or Summer School: Session 1 (S1), Session 2 (S2)

iv.—Score: Select one of the three grading systems, a., b., or c., that applies to your school progress report and/or applies to the specific activity.

a.

(O) = Outstanding
(G) = Good
(S) = Satisfactory
(NI) = Needs Improvement
(U) = Unsatisfactory
(I) = Incomplete
(—) = Absent

b.

(A) = 93–100 [percentage score]
(B) = 85–92
(C) = 75–84
(D) = 70–74
(F) = 0–69
(I) = Incomplete
(—) = Absent

c.

(R/P):
R = Correct number of responses.
P = Possible correct number of responses.
(I) = Incomplete
(—) = Absent

| i | ii/ii |
|---|---|
| iii | iv |

Student's Name ____________________ Class __________ Year __________

## MUSIC SELF-IMPROVEMENT CHART (for student use)

a. On the back of this chart write your goal(s) for music class at the beginning of each semester.
b. On a separate sheet record the date and each new music skill you have acquired during the semester.

c. MUSIC SHARE-A-GRAM (date sent to parent)

| | | | | | | |
|---|---|---|---|---|---|---|
| | | | | | | |

d. RETURN-A-GRAM (date returned to teacher)

| | | | | | | |
|---|---|---|---|---|---|---|
| | | | | | | |

e. MUSIC AWARD BADGES (date and type rec'd)

| |
|---|
| 1. |
| 2. |
| 3. |

f. SPECIAL MUSIC RECOGNITION (date and type rec'd)

| |
|---|
| 1. |
| 2. |
| 3. |

g. SPECIAL MUSIC EVENT ATTENDANCE RECORD (date and name of special performance, recital, rehearsal, concert, field trip, film, workshop, seminar, institute, etc.)

| |
|---|
| 1. |
| 2. |
| 3. |
| 4. |

h. ABOVE AND BEYOND: Extra Credit Projects (date and name of book report, classroom performance, construction of hand-made instrument, report on special music performance on TV, etc.)

| |
|---|
| 1. |
| 2. |
| 3. |
| 4. |

i. PROGRESS REPORT/REPORT CARD RECORD (semester and grade received)

| 1. | 2. | 3. | 4. |
|---|---|---|---|

j. MUSIC SIGN-OUT RECORD (name of instrument, music, book or equipment with sign-out date and due date)

| | | |
|---|---|---|
| 1. | | |
| 2. | | |
| 3. | | |
| 4. | | |
| 5. | | |

| | | |
|---|---|---|
| 6. | | |
| 7. | | |
| 8. | | |
| 9. | | |
| 10. | | |